W9-BCF-885

 INTERFACES

Series Editor: Barbara Green, O.P.

Inquiring of Joseph

Getting to Know a Biblical Character
through the Qur'an

John Kaltner

A Michael Glazier Book

LITURGICAL PRESS

Collegeville, Minnesota

www.litpress.org

A Michael Glazier Book published by the Liturgical Press

Cover design by Ann Blattner. Watercolor by Ethel Boyle.

1   2   3   4   5   6   7   8

Library of Congress Cataloging-in-Publication Data

Kaltner, John, 1954–
    Inquiring of Joseph : getting to know a biblical character through the Qurʾan / John Kaltner.
        p. cm.— (Interfaces)
    "A Michael Glazier book."
    Includes bibliographical references.
    ISBN 0-8146-5153-4 (alk. paper)
    1. Joseph (Son of Jacob) 2. Bible. O.T. Genesis—Criticism, interpretation, etc. 3. Koran—Criticism, interpretation, etc. I. Title. II. Interfaces (Collegeville, Minn.)

BS580.J6K35 2003
222'.11092—dc21

                                                2003046639

CONTENTS

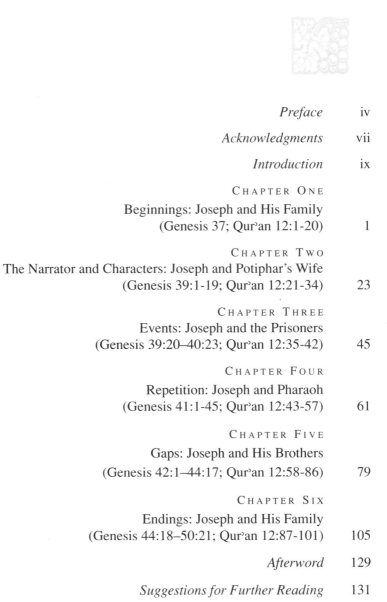

PREFACE

The book you hold in your hand is one of six volumes in a new set. This series, called INTERFACES, is a curriculum and scholarly adventure, a creative opportunity in teaching and learning, presented at this moment in the long story of how the Bible has been studied, interpreted, and appropriated.

The INTERFACES project was prompted by a number of experiences that you, perhaps, share. When I first taught undergraduates the college had just received a substantial grant from the National Endowment for the Humanities, and one of the recurring courses designed within the grant was called Great Figures in Pursuit of Excellence. Three courses would be taught, each centering on a figure from some academic discipline or other, with a common seminar section to provide occasion for some integration. Some triads were more successful than others, as you might imagine. But the opportunity to concentrate on a single individual—whether historical or literary—to team teach, to make links to another pair of figures, and to learn new things about other disciplines was stimulating and fun for all involved. A second experience that gave rise to the present series came at the same time, connected also with undergraduates. It was my frequent experience to have Roman Catholic students feel quite put out about taking "more" biblical studies since, as they confidently affirmed, they had already been there many times and done it all. That was, of course, not true; as we well know, there is always more to learn. And often those who felt most informed were the least likely to take on new information when offered it.

A stimulus as primary as my experience with students was the familiarity of listening to friends and colleagues at professional meetings talking about the research that excites us most. I often wondered: Do her undergraduate students know about this? Or how does he bring these ideas—clearly so energizing to him—into the college classroom? Perhaps some of us have felt bored with classes that seem wholly unrelated to research, that rehash the same familiar material repeatedly. Hence the idea for this series of books to bring to the fore and combine some of our research interest with our teaching and learning. Accordingly, this series is not so much about creating texts *for* student audiences, but rather about *sharing* our scholarly passions with them. Because these volumes are intended each as a piece of original scholarship they are geared to be stimulating to both students and established scholars, perhaps resulting in some fruitful collaborative learning adventures.

The series also developed from a widely-shared sense that all academic fields are expanding and exploding, and that to contemplate "covering" even a testament (let alone the whole Bible or Western monotheistic religions) needs to be abandoned in favor of something with greater depth. At the same time the links between our fields are becoming increasingly obvious as well, and we glimpse exciting possibilities for ways of working that will draw together academic realms that once seemed separate. Finally, the spark of enthusiasm that almost always ignites when I mention to colleagues and students the idea of single figures in combination—interfacing—encourages me that this is an idea worth trying.

And so with the leadership and help of Liturgical Press Academic Editor Linda Maloney, as well as with the encouragement and support of Managing Editor Mark Twomey, the series has begun to take shape.

Each volume in the INTERFACES series focuses clearly on a biblical character (or perhaps a pair of them). The characters are in some cases powerful (King Saul, Pontius Pilate) and familiar (John the Baptist, Joseph) though in other cases they will strike many as minor and little-known (the Cannibal Mothers, Herodias). In any case, each of them has been chosen to open up a set of worlds for consideration. The named (or unnamed) character interfaces with his or her historical-cultural world and its many issues, with other characters from biblical literature; each character has drawn forth the creativity of the author, who has taken on the challenge of engaging many readers. The books are specifically designed for college students (though we think suitable for some graduate work as well), planned to provide young adults with relevant information and at a level of critical sophistication that matches the rest of the undergraduate curriculum. In fact, the expectation is that what students are learning in other classes on historiography, literary theory, and cultural anthropology will find an echo in these books, each of which is explicit about at least two relevant methodologies. It is surely the case that biblical studies is in a methodology-conscious moment, and the INTERFACES series embraces it enthusiastically. Our hope is for students (and teachers) to continue to see the relationship between their best questions and their most valuable insights, between how they approach texts and what they find there. The volumes go well beyond familiar paraphrase of narratives to ask questions that are relevant in our era. At the same time the series authors have each dealt with the notion of the Bible as Scripture in a way that is comfortable for them. None of the books is preachy or hortatory, and yet the self-implicating aspects of working with the revelatory text are handled frankly. The assumption is, again, that college can be a good time for students to rethink their beliefs and assumptions, and they need to do so in good company.

The INTERFACES volumes are not substitutes for the Bible. In every case they are to be read with the text. Quoting has been kept to a minimum for that very reason. The volumes, when used in a classroom setting, are accompanied by a companion volume, *From Earth's Creation to John's Revelation: The INTERFACES Biblical Storyline Companion,* which provides a quick, straightforward overview of the whole storyline into which the characters under special study fit. Web links will also be available through the Liturgical Press website: www.litpress.org.

The series challenge—for publisher, writers, teachers, and students— is to combine the volumes creatively, to "interface" them well so that the vast potential of the biblical text continues to unfold for all of us. The first six volumes: in Old Testament/Hebrew Bible featuring Saul, the Cannibal Mothers, and Joseph; in New Testament focusing on John the Baptist, Herodias, and Pontius Pilate, offer a foretaste of other volumes currently in preparation. It has been a pleasure, and a richly informative privilege, to work with the authors of these first volumes as well as the series consultants: Carleen Mandolfo for Hebrew Bible and Catherine Murphy for New Testament. It is the hope of all of us that you will find the series useful and stimulating for your own teaching and learning.

Barbara Green, O.P.
INTERFACES Series Editor
June 29, 2002
Berkeley, California

ACKNOWLEDGMENTS

This book, which is primarily aimed at an undergraduate audience, first began to take shape inside an undergraduate classroom. During the Spring 2002 semester I taught a course at Rhodes College titled "The Joseph Story in the Bible and the Qur'an," an experience that has been one of the high points of my teaching career. The twenty-three students who took the course committed themselves to a serious and detailed (I am sure at times they thought it was *too* detailed) study of the Joseph story. I dedicate this book to them in appreciation for their hard work, enthusiasm, and patience. It is truly the result of a collaborative effort, although I claim sole responsibility for any shortcomings it contains.

Among those students I would like to recognize Mr. Ambar Paranjape in a special way. During that same semester he was writing a Senior Seminar paper that compared the Joseph and Moses narratives in the Hebrew Bible. He shared that work with me and I found it to be an interesting and insightful paper that influenced my thinking on how the Joseph story is structured.

I wish to extend a final word of thanks to Professor Barbara Green and the Rev. Dr. Linda Maloney of the Liturgical Press for their encouragement and helpful feedback during the writing process. I am very pleased and honored that they have accepted this book for the INTERFACES series.

To the students of RS 300 "The Joseph Story in the Bible and the Qur'an"

David Abney
Constance Baugh
Abby Bomar
Lauren Browder
Stephanie Cox
Matt Crockett
Adam Cromer
Jenna Groner
John Hamilton
Jenny Jordan
Mark Loeffler
Vinay Madan
Anne Mazyck
Shawn McCarthy
Ben McKenzie
Ambar Paranjape
John Ramsey
Eric Swindle
Kathryn Taylor
Natalie Tiner
Sarah Tipton
Adam Underwood
Brian Waggenspack

INTRODUCTION

The account of Joseph and his family that is found in Genesis 37–50 is one of the best-known stories in the entire Bible. It is an extended narrative that traces the fall and rise of a young man from Canaan who literally bottoms out in a well only to attain a position of such power and prominence that people from all over the world come to Egypt to grovel at his feet. Along the way Joseph finds himself in some tight spots and compromising situations that rival anything Indiana Jones ever encountered.

It's your classic rags-to-riches plot with enough twists and turns to satisfy the cravings of the most well-read mystery novel fan. Like all good stories, Joseph's explores themes that have troubled and titillated people throughout history and into our own day. What distinguishes it from most of them is the wide range of such topics it treats in a relatively brief text. Murder, adultery, power, betrayal, sibling rivalry, greed, natural disaster, and mistaken identity are all prominently featured in this story, which presents Joseph as the ultimate survivor. This is the stuff television miniseries are made of, although at times it seems that a soap opera might be a more appropriate vehicle to portray the events of Joseph's life.

To put it simply, it is a great story because it addresses issues that concern us all and it does so in a way that is engaging and memorable. In this book we will consider how and why the story of Joseph and his family has such a powerful effect on its readers. We will do this by employing some of the methods commonly used by Bible scholars and others who analyze texts. In particular, we will make use of approaches that have proved to be helpful in the study of works, like the Joseph story, that are written in narrative form. Comparative analysis is a method commonly employed by Bible scholars that has been quite helpful in determining both what the Bible shares in common with literature from other times and places and what is distinctive or unique about it. Another approach we will utilize is called narrative criticism, which attempts to study how stories are composed and the various elements that comprise them. When we read the Joseph story with the tools provided by comparative analysis and narrative criticism we are in a position to answer some of the questions typically raised by rhetorical criticism, a third methodology that will inform the approach adopted throughout this book. One of the primary aims of rhetorical analysis is to discover how a text attempts to persuade its reader to think a certain way about the characters and events of the story. The following chapters will show how an attentive reading of the text that makes use of these methodologies—comparative analysis, narrative criticism, and rhetorical criticism—can enhance the reader's understanding and enjoyment of the Joseph story.

A Tale of Two Josephs: Comparative Analysis

Since the nineteenth century many texts from ancient Near Eastern cultures have been discovered, deciphered, and compared to sections of the Bible. The majority of these texts have come from Mesopotamia, Egypt, and Canaan, and most of them predate the biblical material. An underlying assumption of scholars' attempts to read these texts in light of the Bible is that they can somehow allow us to better understand the biblical literature. The results of these efforts have varied, depending on the nature of the extra-biblical evidence and the methods (and, sometimes, the personal agendas) of the scholars studying them.

On rare occasions texts have been unearthed that are almost word-for-word parallels to what is contained in the Bible. An example of this can be seen in Prov 22:17–24:34, a collection of wisdom sayings closely mirrored in the Egyptian work "The Instruction of Amenemope" from around 1100 B.C.E. Most of the time the relationships between the Bible and other ancient Near Eastern writings are less obvious, but the latter often still prove very useful to Bible scholars. They can provide valuable information regarding the contexts out of which the Bible emerged, the genres of writing found within it, the themes it treats, and even the meanings of obscure Hebrew words. Biblical laws, prophetic texts, creation accounts, royal annals, and wisdom literature are just a few of the many types of biblical literature that have benefited from such comparative analysis.

By way of illustration we can cite a few well-known examples of the impact this kind of study has had on the field of biblical studies. Both the biblical story of creation that is found in Gen 1:1–2:4a and the account of Noah and the Flood (Genesis 6–9) have often been compared to Mesopotamian texts discovered in the nineteenth century that are much older than the biblical material. In the view of some scholars these ancient Near Eastern texts contain some provocative parallels to the Genesis versions of the events that raise important questions about the origin and background of the biblical accounts.

In 1928 a trove of texts and other material dating back to the fourteenth century B.C.E. was discovered in northern Canaan and immediately had an impact on biblical scholarship. The texts were written in a previously unknown language that was given the name Ugaritic (from the city-state of Ugarit where they were found) and proved to be from the same linguistic family as Hebrew. The close philological and grammatical links between the two languages have made the corpus of Ugaritic writings a valuable tool in understanding problematic Hebrew words and structures that had been troubling Bible scholars for generations. In addition, the Ugaritic texts provided remarkably detailed information on the nature of Canaanite religion during the period when Israelite religion began to emerge in the same general area. For the first time scholars had background information on the worship of Canaanite deities mentioned in the Bible like Baal and El, and they could better understand the context in which Israelite religion began to take shape.

As noted, most of these texts from the ancient Near East were produced before the various works that now comprise the Hebrew Bible were written down and eventually, at a much later date, collected together. Scholars have long debated when the different sections of the Hebrew Bible were written and how they were given their final shape in the form we have today. But most agree that even the oldest portions of the text (the issue of exactly which portions these are is not completely settled) were composed centuries after some of the ancient Near Eastern material to which the Bible has been compared.

There is also a sizeable body of material that is contemporaneous with or later than the Hebrew Bible and that has been studied in light of it and compared to it. Most of these sources are of Jewish origin and can therefore be designated as "biblically affiliated" to distinguish them from other ancient Near Eastern writings that come from contexts that are culturally, chronologically, and theologically farther removed from the Hebrew Bible. Many of these writings, like the midrashim and the Talmud, come from the rabbis. The term *"midrashim"* refers to those rabbinic writings that treat passages of the Hebrew Bible by commenting on them and often adding to them by filling in gaps in the text or answering the questions and solving the problems the texts raise. The Talmud (there are actually two versions, one that originated in Palestine in the fifth century C.E. and the other from Babylon about a century later) is a collection of rabbinic commentary on Jewish law, including legal material found in the Hebrew Bible. Both the midrashim and the Talmud are regularly consulted by Bible scholars as they attempt to understand and interpret the biblical material.

Various translations and versions of the biblical text are also frequently studied and compared to one another. One of the main texts of comparison is the Septuagint, a Greek translation of the Hebrew Bible that was done in Alexandria, Egypt in the third century B.C.E. It is not an exact word-for-word translation of the Hebrew text since significant differences exist between the two versions. In places the Septuagint includes material not present in the Hebrew text and elsewhere it leaves out entire sections of it. One of the most interesting examples of this can be seen in the book of Jeremiah, whose length is about one-eighth shorter in the Greek version than it is in the Hebrew.

A similar phenomenon can be observed in the Dead Sea Scrolls, a cache of biblical and non-biblical writings whose discovery in the 1940s is considered by many to be the greatest archaeological find of the twentieth century. Among the fragments and manuscripts found at the Dead Sea are the oldest examples of biblical texts in existence. When these versions are compared to what is written in the Bible as we have received it, many differences, some of them quite significant, can be observed. Study of how the biblical material compares to the evidence found in the Septuagint, the Dead Sea Scrolls, and versions written in other languages often raises some very important questions about the formation and transmission of the Bible.

As this brief survey suggests, the practice of comparing the Bible with other writings, both "foreign" and closer to home, has a long history within biblical scholarship. There is another body of biblically affiliated material that is less frequently studied. In fact, most people are shocked to discover that it has any association with the Bible whatsoever. I am referring to the Qurʾan, the sacred text of Islam, which is the faith of more than one billion people throughout the world today. Non-Muslims, especially Jews and Christians, are often quite surprised to discover that the Qurʾan has much in common with the Bible, but there is no denying that this is the case. Of particular interest to us is the fact that the Qurʾan frequently refers to figures mentioned in the Bible and contains many stories associated with these characters that are clear parallels to biblical traditions. Adam, Noah, Abraham, Moses, Mary the mother of Jesus, and Jesus himself are among those who play prominent roles in Islam's sacred text. Another biblical character who is featured in the Qurʾan is Joseph, whose story will be the focus of our attention.

How this material ended up in the Qurʾan is a question whose answer depends on who is doing the asking. According to Muslims the Qurʾan is the verbatim word of God (*allah* in Arabic) that was communicated to the prophet Muhammad through the agency of the angel Gabriel in seventh-century C.E. Arabia. It renders all prior revelations, like the Bible, obsolete and is meant to serve as a guide for all humanity. One of the recurring themes throughout the text is the need for people to submit (in Arabic, *islām*) to Allah's will, and the one who does so is called a *muslim*. That same message was sent to prior prophets like the biblical ones mentioned above, but their followers distorted it and did not preserve it in its authentic form. This necessitated the sending of a final prophet, Muhammad, with the definitive and unaltered form of the message (the Qur'an) that serves as a corrective to all previous versions.

For Muslims, then, the presence of "biblical" stories in their text is to be expected since Allah has spoken to these prior prophets and figures of the past. But they consider the Qur'an's account to be the only accurate one. In those places where the Bible conforms to the contents and message of their text it is legitimate divine revelation. But where it differs we have an indication of those places where the Bible was tampered with and distorted.

This is, of course, not how Jews and Christians understand the relationship between the Qur'an and the Bible. In fact, many of them find the Muslim view of the Bible to be an insult and affront to their faith. Some Bible readers hurl the charge of distortion back at the Qur'an and claim that the Islamic text is derivative or a product of Muhammad's fertile imagination. Others have gone to the extreme of maintaining that the Qur'an is the work of the devil. Not all Jewish and Christian assessments of the relationship between the two books have been negative. Some have preferred to focus on the similarities between the Bible and the Qur'an and the opportunities they present for dialogue and mutual understanding among the members of the monotheistic faiths. Others see the lack of agreement in the two texts as evidence of the way God speaks in different ways to people in different contexts.

However one chooses to understand the shared stories in the Qur'an and the Bible, their presence in the two books holds the potential for a positive outcome. It can allow believers from each side to learn something about the beliefs and worldview of the other side while simultaneously learning something about their own. Just as reading texts from the ancient Near East can help improve our understanding of the Bible, so too can a consideration of the way the Qur'an tells the stories increase our appreciation of the forms they take in their biblical context. That is a basic premise of this book, and it is the main reason why we will engage in a comparative analysis of the Joseph story in the Qur'an and the Bible. We are not interested in the question of who got the story right and who got it wrong. Rather, our concern is with the different ways the two books tell the tale and the impact this difference has on the reader.

The Joseph story in the Qur'an is unusual for a couple of reasons. It takes up virtually the entirety of chapter 12 in the Islamic text, the only one of the book's 114 chapters that comprises a single narrative. In addition, at about one hundred verses it is the longest narrative the Qur'an contains. The overall plot of the Islamic version mirrors that of the biblical one, but, as is the case with all the stories the two books share, there are some significant differences between them. When we put the two of them side by side, as we will be doing, the story clearly becomes a tale of two Josephs. He and the other characters often speak and act in noticeably different ways in the two accounts. This has an impact on how the reader experiences the story and the lessons he or she takes away from it. A comparative analysis that puts the Bible and the Qur'an in conversation with each other enables us to recognize the differences between the accounts and also sheds light on aspects of each that we might normally miss. An approach that employs the tools of narrative criticism is the most effective means of realizing that goal. Before we discuss that methodology, a few final comments on the Qur'an are in order.

This book does not pretend to be an introduction to the Qur'an. It is my hope that you will learn some things about Islam's sacred text after reading this book, but what you learn will be just the tip of the proverbial iceberg. A more complete introduction to the Qur'an can be attained by consulting some of the books listed in the bibliography at the end. It is also not my intent to give you a false sense of the contents of the Qur'an. While narrative is found throughout the book and biblical figures play an important role in it, most of the text is quite different in tone and content from what you will be exposed to here. The best way to complete the picture, of course, is to read more of the Qur'an, and some English editions are recommended in the bibliography.

As stated above, the Qur'an's Joseph story can allow us to read and think about its more familiar Genesis counterpart from a fresh perspective. Equally important is the opportunity it provides for non-Muslims to learn something about Islam, the most misunderstood religion in the world. Contrary to what many people think, Islam is a religion of peace that does not teach its followers to hate the members of other faiths. It has a great deal in common with the other monotheistic traditions, but adherents of all three religions typically spend far too much time focusing on what divides them and fail to appreciate all they have in common. At no time in history has an acknowledgment of our shared heritage as children of Abraham been more necessary than it is now. It is my hope that the experience of looking at Joseph through Joseph's eyes might serve as a model for interreligious dialogue among Muslims, Christians, and Jews.

Seeing the Big Picture: Narrative Criticism

In recent decades it has become increasingly common for scholars to read and analyze biblical stories as just that: stories. When critical study of the Bible began to take shape in the eighteenth century the primary emphasis was placed on getting behind the text to understand its origin and formation. Consequently, a great deal of attention was paid to matters like the possible sources, likely authors, and originating contexts of the material that comprises the Bible. This had the effect of causing scholars to think of the Bible and the individual books within it primarily as collections of discrete and separate works. The names of some of the methods that emerged as a result of this approach—source criticism, form criticism, redaction criticism (which studies the editorial process of combining sources)—reflect this view of the biblical material.

Studying the text in this way, often referred to as the historical-critical method, has proved to be a success because it has increased our understanding of the complex nature of the Bible. But, like all approaches, it has its limitations. One of the drawbacks is that it does not always pay sufficient attention to the text as a whole since many of the questions the historical-critical method seeks to address concern the prehistory of the text. In other words, this method is often more interested in the process of how the Bible came to be than in the final product. To use an analogy from the world of art, Bible scholars can sometimes be like a person who stands before a painting and is fixated by the individual colors but fails to appreciate how they all fit together to create an object of beauty. The big picture is missed.

More recently other approaches have been developed that attempt to take in the big picture and are less interested in how biblical texts reached the form in which we now have them. These approaches do not ask questions about the possible sources behind a text or how those sources were edited together. They are concerned only with the end result of that editorial process and ask questions about the text as we have it, as it is read and experienced by people.

Narrative criticism is one of these newer approaches. Since the middle of the twentieth century biblical scholars have begun to draw upon the methods and insights of scholars who study other bodies of literature such as novels, folk tales, and works of mythology. As they have applied to the biblical material what they have learned from these literary critics, new ways of studying and interpreting the Bible have emerged. Rhetorical criticism, reader-response criticism, structuralism, and narrative criticism are some of the major approaches that have emerged within biblical scholarship as a result of this collaboration.

This way of studying the Bible makes sense the more one thinks about it. It might seem strange to some to refer to parts of a sacred text like the Bible as "stories," but that is exactly what they are. In fact, story, or narrative, is the form that dominates a significant portion of the Bible. Why not study that material with the tools that have proved to be most effective for that task even if those tools were initially designed for non-biblical litera-ture? To refuse to do so would be like refusing to attach a keyboard to a computer because keyboards were originally created for typewriters.

Narrative criticism is primarily interested in how stories are structured and arranged. It pays attention to the elements of a narrative that serve as its building blocks and give it shape. Like all forms of literature, stories make use of certain conventions and literary devices that are employed by the au-thor in order to communicate with the reader. Narrative criticism studies how these various aspects function in a given story. This book discusses some of the major elements of narratives as they are found in the Joseph story in the Qurʾan and the Bible. The story will be divided into sections and each chapter will focus on certain elements of the narrative. They will be treated in the following order: (1) how a story begins; (2) the narrator's role and characterization; (3) events and the use of time; (4) repetition; (5) gaps; and (6) how a story ends.

A detailed treatment of each of these elements for each section of the story is not possible here. A particular aspect of narrative criticism is the focus of each chapter, but other aspects that are more fully discussed in other chapters are regularly mentioned and considered. Another way of saying this is that there is an adaptable and interchangeable dimension to the relationships among the chapters. For example, the episode in which the master's wife attempts to seduce Joseph (Chapter Two) is analyzed from the point of view of the narrator's role and characterization, while the description of Joseph's time in prison (Chapter Three) focuses on events and the use of time. The reader is encouraged to reverse the two and apply to one section of the story the methodological principles discussed in the treatment of the other. How does the narrator function in the prison scene? How is time presented in the seduction scene? This kind of approach to the material will allow the reader to gain some practical experience of how narrative criticism works and should lead to some interesting results and fascinating classroom discussion.

By singling out narrative criticism and using it exclusively in this study of the Joseph story, I do not want to give the impression that I think the historical-critical method is unnecessary or irrelevant. Just the opposite is the case. In my view that approach has proved to be an extremely valuable tool in the task of analyzing biblical material and it will continue to make important contributions to the field. But it is only one of several tools, each of which approaches the text in a unique way by asking a different set of questions. In this book we will be asking the questions that narrative criti-cism brings to a text, but they are not the only questions worth asking. Sometimes they are not even the first or most important questions we should ask. For the study of a body of literature that is as diverse and complex as the Bible multiple approaches are needed. The reader who is able to study the text from different perspectives is in a better position to appreciate that richness and complexity.

The relationship between Genesis 38 and the rest of the Joseph story is a notoriously difficult issue to resolve. After the description of Joseph being sold into Egypt by his brothers in chapter 37 there is an abrupt shift to a story about Judah (one of Joseph's brothers) and an improper relationship he has with his daughter-in-law Tamar. Chapter 39 then resumes the Joseph story and opens by repeating the statement found at the end of chapter 37 that he was sold to an Egyptian official named Potiphar. Scholars have disagreed about the connection between the Joseph story and the interlude involving Judah and Tamar. Some see it as an insertion that intrudes and has very little to do with the Joseph story as a whole. Others have maintained that there are a number of thematic and vocabulary links between the two that suggest the Judah/Tamar episode is, in fact, an integral part of the story of Joseph.

In this book the former view will be followed for a couple of reasons. In the first place, the Judah/Tamar material disrupts the flow of the Joseph story despite the presence of elements that are echoed elsewhere in Genesis 37–50. Our analysis will employ the tools of narrative criticism to analyze the Joseph story and there is no reason to treat material that does not advance or contribute to that story in any substantive way. The chapter dealing with Judah and Tamar is a fascinating narrative that deserves careful study, but its relevance for our purposes is minimal. A second reason why we will not be considering Genesis 38 is that it has no counterpart in the Qur'an and therefore cannot be the subject of a comparative analysis. The lack of a parallel story in the other text does not automatically exclude a consideration of it. In fact, we will see that the Qur'an, too, contains a scene that is unique to it, and it will be discussed in some detail in Chapter Two. But when we compare it to the Judah/Tamar material we can see an important difference. The story of the dinner party that the wife of Joseph's master has for the women of the city is well integrated into the Qur'an's version of the story and it has a significant bearing on how the plot develops. It therefore deserves scrutiny in a way that the Judah/Tamar story does not.

The translation of the biblical text used throughout the book is that of the New Revised Standard Version (NRSV). The translation of the Qur'an's Joseph story is my own, and a few brief comments about it are in order. Arabic, like Hebrew, is a highly gendered language in which the grammatical distinction between masculine and feminine is apparent in words other than nouns and pronouns. This is different from a language like English where, for example, the verb "speaks" remains gender free until a subject is attached to it. In Arabic there are two separate forms of the verb depending on whether the one doing the speaking is male or female. In the Qur'an all words that refer to or describe Allah are masculine in gender, and I have translated them into English accordingly in order to give the reader as accurate and literal a sense of the text as possible. But this should not lead to the mistaken assumption that Muslims envision the deity as a male. As an aniconic religion, Islam forbids any attempt to depict or visually represent Allah. To do so would be to engage in *shirk,* or association, the worst sin a person can commit and the only offense that cannot be forgiven. To ascribe a human trait like maleness to Allah would be an example of this because it would associate a quality from the created world with the uncreated divine nature and therefore limit it. According to traditional Muslim belief, the deity is completely transcendent and unknowable to human beings. As is commonly the case with other languages, the limitations of certain features of Arabic, in this case its use of gender, often make it ill-equipped to communicate the subtleties and nuances of theological belief.

When comparing the accounts of the Joseph story in the Bible and the Qur'an I have followed the practice of referring to the deity as "Allah" when discussing the Islamic text and as "God" when treating Genesis. By doing so I am not implying that the two terms refer to separate and distinct deities. The Qur'an and Muslim faith insist that the God of Islam is the God of the Bible, and I do not mean to challenge or undermine that belief. The terms are used in order to help avoid confusion on the reader's part: this terminology distinguishes between the two texts so that they can be more easily and accurately compared.

Reading a text in translation is always fraught with problems. It is very much an experience of "being on the outside, looking in" because a translation, no matter how good, is never able to capture the total essence of the original. There is a definite truth in the old adage that something is always lost in a translation. When it comes to the Qur'an, the first thing that is usually lost is one of the text's most distinctive features, its poetry. This typically takes the form of a rhyming pattern in which the last word of each verse ends with the same or a similar sound. In the Joseph story this effect is realized by ending almost every verse with the letter *m* or *n* preceded by a long vowel. The result is a string of some one hundred verses that conclude in a similar way with the most common endings being *-ūn, -īn,* and *-īm,* a pattern that cannot be duplicated in translation. The Qur'an's Joseph story therefore has a poetic and sonorous quality that is particularly evident when the text is chanted by someone trained in the art of Qur'an recitation.

The poetic dimension of the text does not mean we should set aside the tools of narrative criticism to study it. This is clearly a story, albeit one that rhymes in its original language, and it is perfectly appropriate to analyze it as such by making use of the best methods at our disposal. This is also an approach that has won favor within the Islamic community. In recent times a number of Muslim scholars have studied the Qurʾan's Joseph story as narrative; some examples of these efforts are listed in the bibliography.

The same disclaimer I put forth earlier when discussing the Qurʾan applies here. This book is not meant to offer a comprehensive treatment of narrative criticism. It is an attempt to introduce the reader to the method and the potential it has to facilitate our understanding of stories like that of Joseph. The essentials of narrative criticism are covered, but much more could be said about them as well as about other aspects of the approach. Several very fine works that give a more detailed presentation of the method are available and they, too, are listed in the bibliography.

Joseph Meets Joseph: Rhetorical Criticism

A comparative analysis of the Joseph story in the Qurʾan and the Bible that is informed by narrative criticism allows us to come to a fuller understanding of the rhetorical dimension of the two texts. Many authors write with a desire to do more than simply entertain or communicate information to their audience. They often attempt to influence their readers by convincing them to think a particular way after having read their work. For example, it could be that the author wishes to alter the reader's view of some important individual or event. Or it might be that the author wants the reader to change his or her opinion about some topic.

Rhetorical criticism studies how authors attempt to persuade their readers. The different ways authors go about this task can be easily illustrated by picking up a newspaper and comparing the front page to the editorial page. At first glance the front page appears to be nothing but a set of articles that simply communicate the nuts and bolts of stories without any explicit attempt to influence the reader's perception of what happened. But that is not the case at all. Each article is the result of conscious decisions by the author regarding what gets reported, how it gets reported, and what gets left out of the story. Each of these decisions has an impact on the reader's perception of and reaction to the article, but it is easy for this aspect of the story to escape our notice since it is presented as "objective reporting."

When you open up the editorial page it is impossible to miss the hand and the agenda of the writer. Here is where the author shares his or her opinion and attempts to convince the readers that they should be of the same mind. The writer says, "here's what I think, and if you have any brains at all you'll think the same way." It is a much more overt and blatant form of persuasion than what is found on page one.

Stories of a religious nature like those found in the Bible and the Qur'an usually attempt to persuade their readers, but the form this takes is often closer to that of the front page than it is to the editorial page. There is no denying the fact that parts of the Bible and the Qur'an read like the most aggressively opinionated editorials, but the narratives in the books tend to exhibit a subtler rhetoric that is less pronounced. The Joseph story is a case in point. Although its attempts to influence the reader are sometimes apparent, more often than not they are less obvious and can easily escape detection. Only careful analysis that pays attention to the clues can allow us to get a sense of the author's rhetorical intent.

A comparative approach that adopts the method of narrative criticism is an excellent way to achieve this goal. When the differences between the two versions are noted and studied, the agenda and focus of each becomes clear. In effect, we can more easily see what it is that the author wants us to think about the events and characters of the story. In the same way, the tools of narrative criticism enable us to understand how each story makes use of the conventions of storytelling in its effort to persuade the reader.

Many others have written on the Joseph story in both the Bible and the Qur'an, and some of the most relevant works can be found in the list of suggested readings. I have learned a great deal from consulting these writings, but I have avoided direct reference to them throughout the course of this book. The primary reason for this decision is that I want to keep the focus squarely on a comparative study of the two texts, an approach that has rarely been attempted. The works cited in the bibliography provide excellent background to the material we will study and the methods we will employ, but none of them puts the Bible and the Qur'an in conversation with each other in a prolonged and detailed way. We will listen in on that conversation in order to see what happens in the encounter between Joseph and Joseph.

To put the matter another way, this book takes quite literally the title of the series to which it belongs: here Joseph "interfaces" with Joseph. His biblical self is put in dialogue with his Qur'anic self and we attempt to monitor the exchange. The same might be said of all the other characters in the story. His father, his brothers, his master's wife, the other prisoners, and Pharaoh all have Islamic counterparts who are similar to, but different from, those found in Genesis. They, too, will interface and the results will often be surprising. But perhaps the most surprising outcome will be the reader's realization that, just as with skinning cats, there's more than one way to tell a story and both are worth reading.

CHAPTER ONE

Beginnings: Joseph and His Family (Genesis 37; Qurʾan 12:1-20)

The opening episode of the Joseph story in both the Bible and the Qurʾan introduces the reader to a family that, in modern parlance, is dysfunctional. Jacob's clan exhibits many of the traits we have come to associate with a household in serious need of counseling. Sibling rivalry, parental favoritism, deception, manipulation, and domestic violence are all part of the plot. By the end of this opening section the reader is left with the image of a house torn asunder in which jealousy and suspicion reign supreme and there is not a healthy relationship to be found.

While they agree on the general shape and outline of the story, the Bible and the Qurʾan tell the tale in distinctive ways. This is a situation that we will be encountering throughout the course of this book. Parallel stories in the two texts usually end up in the same place, but they typically take different routes to arrive at their common destination. Such is the case with this opening scene. Joseph will eventually be fished out of a pit and sent off to Egypt in both accounts, but how and why he ends up there and how the news of his "death" plays back home are presented in markedly different ways.

Attention to these differences and their implications can enable the Bible reader to think about the Joseph story in new and interesting ways. Many people who are familiar with the Bible have spent most of their lives reading and hearing the biblical narratives, and they have become so familiar with them that they think they know the material inside out. In fact, that very air of familiarity often has the opposite effect, since it can prevent the recognition of significant aspects of the text. Stories like Joseph's contain many elements that can easily escape our notice unless we use the proper tools to bring them to the surface.

In this and subsequent chapters we will attempt to engage in that enterprise through comparative study of key scenes of the Joseph story as

1

they are found in the Bible and the Qurʾan. The primary tools and methods of narrative criticism will be employed to help identify the differences between the texts and to explore how the Qurʾan's version might enable us to revisit the Genesis material from a fresh perspective. In this way we may more readily begin to acknowledge and appreciate the rich complexity and nuances of the story of Joseph and his family.

In the Beginning

The Joseph story begins in two very different ways in the Bible and the Qurʾan. The Genesis text starts off with a brief statement that Jacob settled in Canaan and then proceeds to turn its attention to the seventeen-year-old Joseph, who will be the protagonist of the story (37:1-2). As is common in biblical narrative, this information is conveyed through an omniscient narrator who speaks in the third person.

> ¹Jacob settled in the land where his father had lived as an alien, the land of Canaan. ²This is the story of the family of Jacob. Joseph, being seventeen years old, was shepherding the flock with his brothers; he was a helper to the sons of Bilhah and Zilpah, his father's wives; and Joseph brought a bad report of them to their father.

The Qurʾan's narrator is also apparent at the outset, but here that narrator speaks in the first person plural ("We") and focuses first not on the Joseph story but on the book in which it is found.

> In the name of Allah, the merciful, the compassionate. ¹Alif Lam Ra. These are the verses of the clear book. ²We have sent it down as an Arabic recitation so that you might understand. ³We relate to you the best of stories in what We reveal to you in this Qur'an. Prior to it you were among the neglectful ones.

This *sūra,* or chapter of the Qurʾan, begins with the same words that start every other chapter in the book but one: "In the name of Allah, the merciful, the compassionate." After this standard opening, the first three verses function as a general introduction to the chapter that is not directly related to the story of Joseph.

The primary aim of this introduction is to provide information on the nature and purpose of the Qurʾan. But before that the text begins with three mysterious words: Alif, Lam, and Ra. These are the names of three letters of the Arabic alphabet, and their presence has been a matter of debate throughout Islamic history. A number of other chapters begin in the same way by listing Arabic letters, but scholars have been unable to reach a satisfactory answer regarding what function, if any, this serves in the text.

Each of the first three verses of the chapter contains a phrase that describes or defines the Qurʾan. In v. 1 it is referred to as the "clear book," highlighting a central quality of the text that is repeatedly mentioned throughout. There are numerous references in the Qurʾan to its own clarity of meaning and the unambiguous language it contains. The same idea is found in the second verse, but in a more subtle way. There the Qurʾan is referred to as an Arabic recitation. The word "Arabic" is often used to describe the language of the people of Arabia, and that is how it should be understood here. But another meaning commonly found in words associated with the same Arabic root has to do with clarity or plainness, particularly regarding speech.

The word "recitation" in v. 2 is a translation of the Arabic word *qurʾān,* and it captures perfectly the nature of Islam's sacred text. This designation underscores the oral dimension of the Qurʾan, a quality that is not found in the Judeo-Christian tradition where the most common words for the sacred text ("Bible" and "scripture") highlight its written, rather than spoken, form. The Qurʾan, a work of poetry of the first order, is a book meant to be heard, not simply read.

In v. 3 the content of the Qurʾan is described as the "best of stories." This phrase should not be taken literally since large portions of the Qurʾan are not in story form. The chapter on Joseph certainly falls under that category and, in fact, is the most extensive narrative found in the entire text of the Qurʾan. It also contains other stories that relate events in the lives of key figures like Abraham, Moses, and Mary the mother of Jesus, but most of the Qurʾan is didactic or instructional in nature and does not communicate its message by telling stories. The qualification of these stories as "the best" is an important one because it underscores the high regard Muslims should have for the material they read in the Qurʾan.

The use of first-person plural forms such as "we," "us," and "our" when Allah speaks is a common feature of the Qurʾan that appears frequently throughout its version of the Joseph story. This is usually understood as an example of the exalted language sometimes used by those in positions of authority when they are addressing subordinates. In earlier periods this was a common mode of discourse used by important people like kings, queens, and popes when they formally communicated with the public. Whatever its precise purpose in the Qurʾan, it should not be understood as evidence of a multiplicity of gods and therefore an implicit challenge to the monotheistic faith that is central to Islam.

A final aspect of this introductory section of the Qur'an that deserves some comment is the identity of its addressee. It is impossible to detect this in English translation, but the passage is actually directed to two different audiences. The reason why this escapes notice is that English has no way of distinguishing between second-person singular and plural forms. In other words, an English speaker uses the word "you" whether addressing one person or a group of people. This is not the case in Arabic where there are separate words for singular and plural "you" and even a dual form that can be used to address two individuals. To further differentiate, each of these words in Arabic also has a masculine and feminine form, resulting in six distinct ways of saying "you," compared to only one in English.

There is a noticeable shift in addressee between the second and third verses of this passage. In v. 2 it is stated that the Qur'an has been sent down so that "you might understand." In the Arabic text the word "you" here is in the masculine plural form indicating that the audience is a group of people, probably comprising both males and females. This is most likely directed to the readers and hearers of the text, both ancient and modern, who are being instructed about the purpose of the Qur'an's revelation.

The focus narrows considerably in the third verse, where it says "We relate to you the best of stories in what We reveal to you in this Qur'an. Prior to it you were among the neglectful ones." Here, all Arabic references to "you" are in the masculine singular, which means a specific individual is being addressed. These words are meant for the prophet Muhammad in his particular context of seventh-century C.E. Arabia.

Such shifts are a standard feature of the Qur'an, whose addressee often unexpectedly jumps from Muhammad to the community and back again to Muhammad in the space of a few verses. This is an illustration of one of the problems of reading a work in translation, where some of the subtleties of the original text often can go unnoticed.

This brief, three-verse introduction to the chapter has a great deal to say about the nature of the Qur'an and it offers a succinct overview of some of the central Muslim tenets regarding the sacred text. But perhaps the most interesting thing about it is its self-referential quality. Unlike the Bible, the Qur'an frequently speaks about itself to describe its purpose and contents. It is, in a sense, a book that tells its readers what it is and how they should therefore relate to it. In other words, it provides clues and directions for the reader that are normally not found in the Bible.

The Qur'an's version of the Joseph story commences with an introduction that plays an important rhetorical function not found in its biblical counterpart. The repeated references to the divine origin of the text and the need for it to be understood by its human audience reinforce the idea that this is a book that should be taken seriously, read reflectively, and pondered deeply. Its placement at the beginning of this chapter also influences how the reader should understand the events of Joseph's life that are about to be narrated. This tale, one of the "best stories," has been sent down so that we might understand. The Bible reader is provided with no such guidance regarding the nature of the material and how to read it.

Meeting the Players (Genesis 37:3-11; Qur'an 12:4-6)

The old adage that "first impressions are lasting impressions" can be applied to literary characters as well as to flesh-and-blood human beings. The initial encounter with a figure in a story can leave an enduring mark on the reader and exert a great deal of influence on how that character is perceived and evaluated throughout the course of the narrative. To put it another way, the first words and actions of the principal characters in a story often do much to set the tone and give the reader some idea about the future direction of the plot.

This is precisely the situation with the Joseph story in the Bible and the Qur'an. As we listen to what Jacob and his sons have to say to one another and we observe their behavior, we begin to form opinions about what kind of people they are and where their story might be headed. As is often the case when we compare stories in the two texts, the first impressions we are left with vary considerably. The Qur'an, as usual, presents a shorter, more succinct introduction to the family dynamics than the Genesis account offers. What the Islamic text covers in three verses the biblical tradition presents in nine.

> ⁴When Joseph said to his father, "Oh my father, I saw eleven stars, the sun, and the moon—I saw them bow down to me," ⁵he said, "Oh my son, do not relate your vision to your brothers for they will plot against you. Truly, Satan is a clear enemy to people. ⁶Thus, your Lord will choose you, teach you how to interpret events, and confer His favor upon you and upon the family of Jacob just as He conferred it earlier upon your two ancestors Abraham and Isaac. Truly, your Lord is the one who knows, the wise one."

Joseph's father is not explicitly identified as Jacob in this first part of the story in the Qur'an, but we will refer to him by this name since it is quite clear that he is the counterpart of the biblical Jacob. Verses 4 through 6 are in the form of a conversation in which each side has only one line of dialogue. Joseph tells his father about his vision in which eleven stars, the sun, and the moon bow down to him. Jacob cautions his son against telling his brothers about the vision and then reminds him that he must be on guard against Satan, who is humanity's enemy. After this his father goes on to inform Joseph of the many things Allah will do for him.

If we consider Joseph's character in relation to each of the others mentioned in these three verses a general picture of the underlying tensions and issues of the plot begins to emerge. He and Jacob appear to have the kind of relationship that is typical of many fathers and sons. Joseph's vision is an experience that has left him confused, perhaps even troubled, and he mentions it to his father. The older man offers some words of advice meant to encourage and support his child. The closeness and intimacy between them is reflected in the way they address each other as "my father" and "my son."

Joseph's relationship with his brothers is more ambiguous. In the first place, he has chosen to confide in his father about the vision, a choice that might reflect uncertainty about how his brothers could react to it. Second, his father plainly warns Joseph against speaking to his brothers about the vision because it will only lead to hostility against him. At this early point in the narrative the reader has been alerted to potential problems in the family and has begun to form a negative impression of Joseph's brothers even though they have not yet appeared on the scene.

The brothers are not the only figures the reader views suspiciously. Jacob also urges his son to watch out for Satan, who is described as a "clear enemy to people." The mention of Satan immediately after the reference to the plotting of Joseph's brothers is probably meant to link together these two elements. The reader is led to the conclusion that it is ultimately Satan who is responsible for human evil and violence of the sort that the brothers might plan. This does not absolve the brothers of blame, but it identifies the source of their animosity toward Joseph. Satan will return at two critical points in the Joseph story (vv. 42, 100), and his involvement then will validate the father's warning here at the outset of the narrative.

After the double warning about the brothers and Satan, his father then gives Joseph the good news: Allah will be with him and will protect him from harm. The whole of v. 6 is taken up with a description of the deity's excellent qualities and involvement in Joseph's life: Allah will choose Joseph, teach him how to interpret events, and confer favor on him and his entire family. The section ends with a reference to Allah as "the one who knows, the wise one." This description, which will be repeated a number of times throughout the Joseph story in the Qurʾan, highlights the supreme knowledge and wisdom of the deity that will insure success for Joseph and his family.

This introduction to some of the primary players in the story identifies four sets of relationships, two positive and two negative, that will be central to the plot's development and outcome in the Qur'an. On the positive side are Joseph's relationships with his father and Allah. Jacob is someone in whom he can confide and who gives him advice and support when he needs it. Allah, too, will be a constant source of strength and encouragement through the divine favor that will be bestowed on Joseph and his family. On the negative side we have Joseph's relationships with his brothers and Satan. Although not much has been said about them at this point in the narrative, Jacob's words suggest that Joseph and his brothers are not on good terms. The brothers' actions and words will soon make their father's warning seem prophetic. Likewise, the reference to Satan as an enemy of people sounds an ominous note and points to another problematic relationship.

This section also contains the first occurrences of two themes that will recur throughout the Joseph story in the Qur'an. The first is found in v. 5 with the mention of Joseph's brothers plotting against him. The Arabic root found here *(kāda)* can mean "plot, deceive, or beguile" and words based on it are found nine times in this chapter. In this verse it appears twice, since Jacob's words translate literally as "they will plot a plot against you." The nine occurrences of this root in the Joseph story are more than we find in any other chapter of the book. They also account for more than one quarter of the total times it is used in the entire Qur'an. The motif of plotting or deceiving is clearly important to the narrative, and we will see that it plays a prominent role at several key junctures of the story.

The other significant theme first mentioned here is found in v. 6, where one of the titles of Allah is "the one who knows." We will see that knowledge, or its absence, is a critical component of the Qur'an story since words built on the Arabic root *'alima* ("know") are found thirty-two times in the chapter. Such a high concentration of words related to knowledge tells us that we should pay careful attention to them whenever they appear.

The Bible's account of these events is found in Genesis 37:3-11:

> [3]Now Israel loved Joseph more than any other of his children, because he was the son of his old age; and he had made him a long robe with sleeves. [4]But when his brothers saw that their father loved him more than all his brothers, they hated him, and could not speak peaceably to him. [5]Once Joseph had a dream, and when he told it to his brothers, they hated him even more. [6]He said to them, "Listen to this dream that I have dreamed. [7]There we were, binding sheaves in the field. Suddenly my sheaf rose and stood upright; then your sheaves gathered around it, and bowed down to my sheaf." [8]His brothers said to him, "Are you indeed to have dominion over us?" So they hated him even more because of his dreams and his words." [9]He had another dream and

told it to his brothers, saying, "Look, I have had another dream: the sun, the moon, and eleven stars were bowing down to me." ¹⁰But when he told it to his father and to his brothers, his father rebuked him, and said to him, "What kind of dream is this that you have had? Shall we indeed come, I and your mother and your brothers, and bow to the ground before you?" ¹¹So his brothers were jealous of him, but his father kept the matter in mind.

Several elements of the biblical version are not found in the Qur'an. In Genesis, Jacob has a special place in his heart for Joseph as seen in the gift of the coat. The Islamic text makes no mention of this paternal favoritism. Similarly, the Bible records two dreams of Joseph, the second one being virtually identical to the one in the Qur'an referred to as a "vision." A further interesting difference is that Joseph actually relates his dreams to his brothers in Genesis (vv. 5 and 9), while this is not explicitly stated in the Qur'an.

We can also identify aspects of the Qur'an version that are not found in the Bible. For example, the biblical tradition does not refer to God or Satan, two figures who are mentioned in the Qur'an. This lack of any mention of God or Satan means that there is no explicitly theological dimension to this portion of the biblical story of Joseph.

It is when we consider the human characters and how they relate among themselves that we observe some fascinating differences between the two accounts. The overall structure of the two is not the same. We have seen that the Qur'an version is organized around a brief conversation between Joseph and his father. The Genesis one, on the other hand, contains two scenes that describe encounters between Joseph and his brothers, with their father speaking only at the end of the second one. The focus in the Bible, then, is on the relationship Joseph has with his brothers, while in the Qur'an it is his relationship with his father that is primary in the scene.

Joseph's relationship with Jacob is explicitly treated at the beginning and end of the biblical passage. Verse 3 states that Jacob, here identified as Israel, loved Joseph more than any of his other children, and it provides a reason for and a result of this affection. Joseph's special status is due to his having been born late in his father's life, and Jacob's preference for him is expressed in the gift of the special coat meant to be a sign of that love. This reference to Joseph's coat foreshadows other scenes later in the biblical story when his clothing will figure prominently and will usually signal a change in his status, as it does here.

This image of parental love and partiality is challenged at the end of the biblical passage when Jacob reappears. In v. 10 he speaks for the first time in the story when, in reaction to Joseph's second dream, he says, "What kind of dream is this that you have had? Shall we indeed come, I and your mother and your brothers, and bow to the ground before you?" There is a definite edge to these two questions that is reflected in the verse's use of the verb "rebuke" to describe Jacob's reaction. The sharp tone of Jacob's words is particularly apparent when we compare it to his much more positive and affirming response to the same vision in the Qur'an. In the Islamic text Jacob gives Joseph something, but it serves a very different purpose than the coat in Genesis that helps to widen the gulf between Joseph and his brothers. The Jacob of the Qur'an gives him advice meant to lessen the fraternal friction and keep the family from tearing itself apart: "Oh my son, do not relate your vision to your brothers, for they will plot against you." In this text, as in Genesis, Jacob has only one line of dialogue, but here they are words of encouragement and clear instruction to his son rather than the rhetorical questions in the biblical account that put Joseph on the spot.

Jacob's one line of dialogue in each text, then, plays a major role in determining the nature of the father/son relationship. The Joseph of the Bible has the coat to remind him of his favored position, but Jacob's response to his dream gives him cause to wonder about his real status in his father's eyes. In contrast, the coatless Joseph of the Qur'an has Jacob's advice and guidance, which leave no doubt about his father's true feelings.

Genesis presents a more detailed description of Joseph's relationship with his brothers than we find in the Qur'an. The biblical account begins on a positive note with its reference to the seventeen-year-old Joseph tending the flock with his brothers. This image of fraternal harmony and cooperation is called into question at the end of v. 2 with the mention that "Joseph brought a bad report of them to their father." The substance of the report is unidentified, but it raises questions in the reader's mind about Joseph's relationship with the brothers.

The reference to Jacob's preference for Joseph comes immediately after this and is, in turn, followed by a very blunt statement of the enmity his brothers feel toward him. "But when his brothers saw that their father loved him more than all his brothers, they hated him, and could not speak peaceably to him." These negative feelings quickly escalate when v. 5 describes how his brothers come to hate him "even more" after Joseph tells them of his first dream. This same idea is found a few verses later when their reaction to the first dream is repeated: "So they hated him even more because of his dreams and words." The final reference to the brothers in this section comes with the mention of their jealousy in v. 11. There is a clear intensification of their anger throughout these verses that will culminate in the plan they will soon conceive to rid themselves of their younger brother.

This description of the relationship between Joseph and his brothers is one-sided. The reader is told repeatedly what the brothers are thinking and feeling but is never given any information about Joseph's state of mind. Is Joseph aware of his brothers' dislike for him at this point in the story? Does he feel the same way toward them? Is he in any way responsible for their feelings toward him? The Genesis text does not allow us to answer these questions with certainty, but it does contain some clues that enable us to gain limited insight into Joseph's side of the relationship. In the first place, there is the matter of the "bad report" about his brothers that Joseph brings to Jacob in v. 2. Were the brothers doing something dangerous or illegal that deserved to be called to their father's attention? Or was the situation less serious, and was Joseph simply engaging in the time-honored practice of being a tattletale sibling? Did the brothers know Joseph had gone to Jacob with the report? Was his willingness to tell on his brothers another reason why he was his father's favorite son?

These and similar questions exert an influence over how the reader evaluates Joseph's character and his relationship with the brothers. Bringing his father information about his brothers indicates that he is no passive partner in the relationship, and it raises a red flag in the reader's mind suggesting that Joseph may not be a completely innocent victim.

The same thing can be said about the second dream. When Joseph related his first dream to the brothers their reaction was immediate and unambiguous. The reader does not know if Joseph was aware of the depth of their hatred toward him at this point, but their disapproval of the dream's apparent meaning was clear and unmistakable. And yet, when he has a second dream whose meaning is more or less the same as that of the first, he runs the risk of further enraging them by telling his brothers about it. Why would Joseph do such a thing, knowing it would, in all probability, only fan the flames of their anger? Whether we attribute this to youthful impulsiveness, spiteful pride, or something else, the reader cannot help but wonder about Joseph's involvement in the degeneration of his fraternal ties. Has he contributed, wittingly or not, to his brothers' hostility and brought this on himself? Whatever the answer, at this point in the biblical narrative Joseph's relationship with his brothers has the air of an accident waiting to happen.

An attempt is made to avert the accident in the Qurʾan: there the brothers are only mentioned once in the passage and never appear on the scene. As a result, Joseph's possible role in the deterioration of his relationship with them is not as apparent in the Islamic text as it is in the Bible. There is no reference to the bad report that is mentioned in Genesis, making Joseph less responsible for any hard feelings that might exist between him and his siblings. When his father speaks of a possible plot by the brothers in the

Qur'an it cannot be linked to anything Joseph has said or done up to this point in the narrative.

Another reason why Joseph is relatively free of blame in the Qur'an is that he does not tell his brothers of his vision and thereby run the risk of provoking their anger. The reader is led to assume that he obeys his father and follows the advice not to speak of the matter. How different this is from the Genesis version of events where Joseph goes to his brothers with the news of a dream and then returns a second time to relate another one to them despite their less than positive response to the first one! The Qur'an, then, lacks the two elements of the biblical plot that most clearly suggest Joseph may have been partly responsible for the situation he will soon find himself facing. By not delivering the bad report to his father and by not telling his brothers about his dream, the Islamic Joseph is less potentially culpable than his biblical counterpart. The assertive sibling of Genesis who just might be a snitch is a compliant, obedient son in the Qur'an.

Who Knows? (Genesis 37:12-36; Qur'an 12:7-19)

[7]In Joseph and his brothers there are signs for those who inquire. [8]They said, "Joseph and his brother are more loved by our father than we are, but we are a large group. Truly, our father is in clear error. [9]Kill Joseph or cast him away to some far land and your father's favor will be yours only. After that you will be a righteous people." [10]One of them said, "Do not kill Joseph. If you must do something, cast him into the bottom of a well where some travelers will come upon him." [11]They said, "Oh our father, why do you not trust us with Joseph? We are his mentors. [12]Send him with us tomorrow so he might enjoy himself and play. We are his guardians." [13]He said, "It concerns me to have him go with you. I fear that a wolf might devour him while you are unmindful." [14]They replied, "If a wolf should devour him, we, large group that we are, will have already perished." [15]When they went out with him they agreed to cast him into the bottom of a well. We revealed to him, "You will surely tell them of this deed of theirs when they will not know." [16]They returned to their father in the evening, crying. [17]They said, "Oh our father, we hastily went off leaving Joseph with our provisions and a wolf devoured him! You will not believe us even though we are telling the truth." [18]They came with false blood on his shirt. He said, "No! Rather, your minds have led you to make up this story. Beautiful patience! Allah is the one whose help is sought against what you have described." [19]Some travelers came and sent their water carrier who let down his bucket and cried, "Good news! A youth!" They hid him as merchandise, but Allah knew what they did.

This section of the Qur'an chapter opens with a comment directed to the reader that is not actually a part of the Joseph story. It communicates something about the nature of the material and how to interpret it. According to v. 7 the characters and events of the narrative function primarily as signs. This term indicates that we should not take the story of Joseph and his brothers simply at face value but we should attempt to uncover its real meaning by discovering the other reality to which it points.

The verse explains how to do this—we should "inquire." If we acknowledge a deeper meaning to the text and ask questions of it, the true meaning behind the story can emerge and instruct us. Once again, the Qur'an provides clues and directions to the reader that are not found in the Bible. Responding to the invitation, we now inquire of the text in order to decipher the signs it contains.

A theme that runs throughout this portion of the Qur'an story concerns the identity of the brothers. In the Arabic text seven of the thirteen verses end with a noun that describes some trait or quality the brothers possess. Six of these occur in rapid succession when vv. 9 through 14 all conclude in this way and contribute to the compilation of a fairly detailed group portrait. In order of occurrence, the brothers are described as righteous, doers, mentors, guardians, unmindful, and perished. In v. 17 the final component of this catalogue of traits refers to them as truthful. Almost all of these terms denote positive qualities and almost all of them are found on the lips of the brothers themselves. The only one not spoken by them is the sole negative trait: their father describes them as unmindful. It is clear that in this passage the brothers go to great lengths to present a comprehensive and unabashedly flattering assessment of their group identity.

Another word the brothers use to identify themselves is the Arabic term *'uṣba,* found twice in this passage, where it is translated as "large group" (vv. 8 and 14). Normally the word refers to a group of individuals who join together for defensive or military purposes, a sense that is clearly operative in v. 14 when the brothers speak of banding together to ward off an attacking wolf.

This meaning is less obvious in v. 8 when they react to the favoritism shown Joseph, but if it is present there it adds a revealing dimension to their statement. Their self-designation as an *'uṣba* in this context could be meant to draw attention to the battle lines that have been drawn within their family and the resulting "us versus them" mentality that is engendered. They have come to view their father's preference for Joseph and his brother as a threat that is as real and serious as that posed by an attacking wolf. In this situation they must join together to defend themselves against the enemy in order to survive.

The brothers' self-image is at odds with their father's understanding of them. The events of the story will show that their father knows them better than they know themselves. Their words and actions implicate the brothers, and this causes the reader to view them in a negative light. Their father's preference for Joseph and his brother suggests to them that the older man is "in error" (v. 8), and this leads them to devise a scheme to rid themselves of their brother. When they refer to themselves as Joseph's mentors and guardians the lie is so transparent that the reader can only conclude that they are manipulating their father into letting them take Joseph with them.

The reader's opinion of the brothers reaches its nadir when they return home with their made-up story and tearfully protest to their father, "You will not believe us even though we are telling the truth." The reader knows all they have done to violate their fraternal and paternal ties: what happens to Joseph is the result of a calculated, premeditated scheme on the part of the brothers. Their actions have condemned them despite their claims to the contrary.

What about Jacob's involvement in this family mess? Is he partly to blame for what happens to Joseph? This is a legitimate question to ask since he has already expressed his concern about a possible plot against Joseph (v. 5) and he voices strong reservations against entrusting him to the care of his brothers (v. 13). Given his apprehension, why would he allow the brothers to be alone with Joseph?

His words when the brothers return without Joseph help to exonerate Jacob of any guilt. He recognizes that the brothers' tears are as phony as the blood they have planted on Joseph's shirt, and he calls upon divine refuge. "No! Rather, your minds have led you to make up this story. Beautiful patience! Allah is the one whose help is sought against what you have described." This is simultaneously an assertion that he has seen through the brothers' charade and an expression of his faith in Allah's power to right the wrong they have committed. At this low point in his life Jacob surrenders all control and authority to Allah, and the reader can reasonably conclude that this same faith is what enabled him to put Joseph into his brothers' care. In reality he was placing him under the care of Allah.

This is not the only time Allah is mentioned in the Qur'an passage. The deity becomes an active character in v. 15 by speaking to Joseph when he has been cast into the well: "You will surely tell them of this deed of theirs when they will not know." Allah defines the brothers as ignorant and is therefore developing what we have seen to be a major element of this part of the Qur'an chapter. But rather than follow their lead and describe them in positive terms, the deity sides with Jacob by highlighting a flaw or deficiency in their character.

We know very little about Joseph up to this point in the story since he never speaks and we are not given any indication of what he is thinking. In fact, the Qur'an text does not even contain an account of how the brothers get rid of him. But this lack of detail does not mean he fails to evoke a strong reaction from the reader. All alone at the bottom of the well after having been ambushed by his brothers, Joseph is an object of pity and sympathy who is clearly an innocent victim in the Islamic text. The only ray of light in the darkness is the comforting message from Allah assuring him that he will survive his ordeal.

Allah's reference to the brothers' lack of knowledge underscores the central theme of this part of the narrative. This is a story about knowledge, both real and imagined. The brothers are know-it-alls. The labels they use to describe themselves and others show that the brothers believe they have a clear understanding of the situation and how to manipulate it to their benefit. Joseph is their father's favorite, but the old man is clearly in error. The brothers construct a glowing image of themselves in order to dupe their father into allowing them to achieve their true goal, the removal of Joseph from their lives.

Despite their smug certainty as they evaluate the situation and concoct their evil scheme, the brothers are in fact hopelessly out of touch and far removed from the source of true knowledge. This is apparent when we compare them to their father and Joseph, who are much more knowledgeable than the brothers even though they do not appear to have the upper hand at this point in the plot. Their knowledge comes from a different source than that of the brothers, which is self-centered and delusional.

Jacob knows the truth. He is able to see right through his sons' machinations and he refuses to accept the lies they tell him. It is primarily his faith in Allah that makes this possible. Earlier in the chapter Jacob expressed his trust and confidence in the deity when he told Joseph that Allah had chosen him and would protect him and his family (v. 6). Still confident of that divine protection, Jacob now rejects his other sons' claim that Joseph has been killed.

Joseph, too, possesses insight that the brothers lack, and he has every reason to be certain of its authenticity. Allah speaks to him directly and assures him that the bottom of the well will not be his final resting place. The brothers do not stand a chance when they pit their knowledge against that of Jacob and Joseph. Unlike their father and brother they neither express faith in Allah nor receive a divine revelation—Allah's description of them as "not knowing" is apt indeed.

Fittingly, the section ends by calling attention to Allah's knowledge. "They hid him as merchandise, but Allah knew what they did." On one level this can be read as a reference to Allah's awareness of what the travelers did in hiding Joseph. But it could also be taken as a more global statement about the deity's complete knowledge of all things, including what the brothers have done by abandoning Joseph and trying to hoodwink their father. In this portion of the chapter in which knowledge plays such a central role this is the only explicit statement that a character knows something.

Ironically, the brothers' efforts to label themselves and others throughout the course of the section are pointless because their identity has been established by the text in v. 7. "In Joseph and his brothers there are signs for those who inquire." Our own inquiry into the narrative has given us some insight into how the characters function as signs. Two types of people are represented in the story, each possessing a different type of knowledge. The brothers symbolize those who think they know it all and do not need to look beyond themselves for help and guidance. They are sure of who they are, and they believe they control their own lives and fate. Joseph and his father symbolize a different kind of person who does not rely solely on this type of knowledge. They represent those who look to Allah for guidance and seek divine help in the midst of difficulty.

The events treated in v. 7 through 19 of the Qur'an's Joseph story are found in Genesis 37:12-36.

> [12]Now his brothers went to pasture their father's flock near Shechem. [13]And Israel said to Joseph, "Are not your brothers pasturing the flock at Shechem? Come, I will send you to them." He answered, "Here I am." [14]So he said to him, "Go now, see if it is well with your brothers and with the flock; and bring word back to me." So he sent him from the valley of Hebron. He came to Shechem, [15]and a man found him wandering in the fields; the man asked him, "What are you seeking?" [16]"I am seeking my brothers," he said; "tell me, please, where they are pasturing the flock." [17]The man said, "They have gone away, for I heard them say, 'Let us go to Dothan.'" So Joseph went after his brothers, and found them at Dothan. [18]They saw him from a distance, and before he came near to them, they conspired to kill him. [19]They said to one another, "Here comes this dreamer. [20]Come now, let us kill him and throw him into one of the pits; then we shall say that a wild animal has devoured him, and we shall see what will become of his dreams." [21]But when Reuben heard it, he delivered him out of their hands, saying, "Let us not take his life." [22]Reuben said to them, "Shed no blood; throw him into this pit here in the wilderness, but lay no hand on him"—that he might rescue him out of their hand and restore him to his father. [23]So when Joseph came to his brothers, they stripped him of his robe, the long robe with sleeves that he wore; [24]and they took him and threw him into a pit. The pit was empty; there was no

water in it. ²⁵Then they sat down to eat; and looking up they saw a caravan of Ishmaelites coming from Gilead, with their camels carrying gum, balm, and resin, on their way to carry it down to Egypt. ²⁶Then Judah said to his brothers, "What profit is it if we kill our brother and conceal his blood? ²⁷Come, let us sell him to the Ishmaelites, and not lay our hands on him, for he is our brother, our own flesh." And his brothers agreed. ²⁸When some Midianite traders passed by, they drew Joseph up, lifting him out of the pit, and sold him to the Ishmaelites for twenty pieces of silver. And they took Joseph to Egypt. ²⁹When Reuben returned to the pit and saw that Joseph was not in the pit, he tore his clothes. ³⁰He returned to his brothers, and said, "The boy is gone; and I, where can I turn?" ³¹Then they took Joseph's robe, slaughtered a goat, and dipped the robe in the blood. ³²They had the long robe with sleeves taken to their father, and they said, "This we have found; see now whether it is your son's robe or not." ³³He recognized it, and said, "It is my son's robe! A wild animal has devoured him; Joseph is without doubt torn to pieces." ³⁴Then Jacob tore his garments, and put sackcloth on his loins, and mourned for his son many days. ³⁵All his sons and all his daughters sought to comfort him; but he refused to be comforted, and said, "No, I shall go down to Sheol to my son, mourning." Thus his father bewailed him. ³⁶Meanwhile the Midianites had sold him in Egypt to Potiphar, one of Pharaoh's officials, the captain of the guard.

The general outline of this passage is quite similar to what is found in the Islamic text, but there are some interesting differences. For example, the idea that Joseph and his brothers are signs is not found in the biblical tradition. This is mainly due to the different purposes of the two books. The Bible, particularly in its narrative sections, is primarily interested in presenting the story of God's relationship and dealings with the chosen people. It adopts a more or less chronological approach as the history of the covenant between the Israelites and their God is recounted.

The Qur'an has a very different agenda. It does not present a chronological rehearsal of salvation history, but opts for an approach that focuses more on the themes or lessons of individual passages. The Islamic book does not start at the beginning, as the Bible does, and then go on to present the history of a particular group of people. It adopts a less structured format as it moves from theme to theme and figure to figure in a way that can strike the Bible reader as haphazard and confusing. Its primary concern is to instruct the reader about particular topics and matters, whereas the Bible's organizing structure is the plot that recounts history in sequential order. In the Qur'an it is the centrality of the message that tends to grab the reader's attention. For this reason, the text informs its readers at the outset that Joseph and his brothers are signs, and this cue prompts the reader regarding how to approach and interpret the text.

There are a number of other obvious differences between the Genesis and Qur'an texts. The biblical scene in vv. 14b-17 that describes Joseph's encounter with a man who helps him find his brothers has no counterpart in the Qur'an. Genesis also contains a couple of examples of what biblical scholars refer to as "doublets," two scenes describing the same event with minor variations in character and/or plot. One instance of this concerns the identity of the brother who pleads for Joseph's life. In vv. 21-22 Reuben convinces his siblings to spare their younger brother, while in vv. 26-27 Judah plays the same role.

Similarly, the identity of the group to which Joseph is sold is not completely clear because two are mentioned. In v. 25 the brothers see a caravan of Ishmaelites to whom Judah suggests they sell Joseph, but then in v. 28 we are told that some Midianites rescue Joseph and sell him to the Ishmaelites who take him to Egypt. The matter is further complicated when v. 36 states that the Midianites sold Joseph in Egypt. Scholars have often explained the presence of such doublets as evidence of different sources behind the biblical text. In the present case some posit the existence of one source that describes Judah and the Ishmaelites as the key actors and another source in which Reuben and the Midianites are mentioned. However one attempts to explain the shape of the biblical tradition, it is clearly a text that is more complicated than the one in the Qur'an, which refers to only one anonymous brother who tries to save Joseph and only one group of travelers, also unnamed.

We have seen that an important element of the Qur'an's version of events is the way it distinguishes between true and false knowledge. This same theme is present in Genesis, but it does not play quite the same role since it does not serve to differentiate the characters. In fact, a careful analysis of the biblical tradition highlights an interesting connection among the characters that helps to shape the plot: they all share in a lack of knowledge.

Jacob is mentioned twice in the Genesis passage under discussion, once at the beginning (vv. 12-14) and once at the end (vv. 32-35). In both these places his lack of knowledge about important matters is apparent. In the earlier scene Jacob sends Joseph to Shechem, where he believes the other brothers are pasturing the flock. The reader is inclined to accept the reliability of this information because v. 12 states that this is in fact where the brothers have gone. But when Joseph arrives at Shechem he cannot find them and wanders around until a stranger tells him his brothers have moved on to Dothan.

This brief episode reveals Jacob's lack of knowledge, since he wrongly assumes his older sons are in one place when they are actually in another. The same might be said about his awareness of Joseph's whereabouts. He assumes his younger son has followed his instructions and is now reunited with his siblings in Shechem, but in truth he has journeyed on to another location. At this point in the narrative Jacob does not know where his children are, and his ignorance is a sign of things to come.

In the later scene (vv. 32-35) Jacob's lack of knowledge is a key motif that contributes a great deal to the drama and pathos of the story. Upon seeing Joseph's bloody robe Jacob is convinced of his son's demise and begins to lament his passing. Throughout the scene that knowledge, misinformed though it is, determines the plot development. The brothers ask him to identify Joseph's robe, and his recognition of it is what triggers the mourning ritual he enacts.

Two aspects of Jacob's words in this section are noteworthy. In the first place, they are all fraught with the emotion that naturally accompanies reaction to the news of the unexpected death of a child. "It is my son's robe! A wild animal has devoured him; Joseph is without doubt torn to pieces. . . . No, I shall go down to Sheol to my son, mourning." A second quality of Jacob's words is that they are, for the most part, entirely untrue. The only utterance that has a basis in fact is his first one: "It is my son's robe!" All the others are errors or faulty conclusions resulting from Jacob's lack of knowledge. According to Genesis, at this point in the narrative Jacob is in the dark about the facts pertaining to his sons. And he will remain there for quite some time.

How different this is from the situation in the Qur'an where Jacob sees right through the brothers' machinations and does not fall for their trick. The knowledge he lacks in Genesis is present in the Islamic text, as is another important quality not found in the Bible: his faith. In Genesis, Jacob is a tragic figure who is completely alone, mourning the death of a still-living son and unable to be consoled by the children yet with him. In the depths of his despair he wants to join his son in death and is unable to call upon divine assistance. The reader cannot imagine him responding to his situation with the words he utters in the Qur'an, "Beautiful patience!"

There are some notable differences in the ways the two texts present Joseph, as well. One concerns the circumstances that lead to his being alone with his brothers. In the Qur'an this is the brothers' doing, since they take the initiative by suggesting Joseph be allowed to accompany them and they continue to pester their father until he gives in to their wish.

In Genesis this is not the way things happen. It is Joseph himself who does all he can to insure that he will be reunited with his brothers. He is so intent on this goal that he travels from Shechem to Dothan, a journey of more than ten miles over fairly difficult terrain, when he discovers they are no longer where his father told him they would be. This is an important difference because it makes the brothers appear less calculating and duplicitous in Genesis than they are in the Qurʾan. They do not devise a trap with which to ensnare their younger brother; Joseph more or less falls into their laps. Ironically, he is partly responsible for this because of the great lengths to which he goes to find them.

The second difference between the two texts is a very important one. In the Bible God never speaks to Joseph in the pit to reassure him. This adds a further element of abandonment to Joseph's character in Genesis. As in the Islamic text, his brothers mistreat him and he might even be questioning the motives of his father who sent him off to be with them. But the biblical Joseph labors under the additional burden of not having the divine encouragement and support his counterpart in the Qurʾan receives. He is not told that he will one day confront his brothers about what they have done to him. The bottom of the pit is a more lonely and terrifying place for Joseph in Genesis than it is in the Qurʾan.

There is, then, an interesting similarity in the ways Joseph and Jacob are presented in the two versions of the story. In the Qurʾan they possess knowledge from Allah that allows them to remain confident and steadfast in the midst of their trials. This element is not a part of the biblical telling of the tale. Joseph, like his father, is totally on his own and lacking any spiritual guidance or assistance in the midst of his ordeal.

An attentive reading of the Genesis text indicates that this pattern holds for the brothers as well. We have already observed how frequently the brothers in the Qurʾan use labels and titles to identify themselves and others in their efforts to control events. Things are different in Genesis, where they never label themselves and the only time they use a title in reference to another person is in v. 19, when they describe Joseph as a "dreamer." But unlike the labels they use in the Qurʾan, this one is appropriate since Joseph is, in fact, a dreamer.

The brothers in the biblical story are not as overtly manipulative as their counterparts in the Qurʾan. They do not persuade their father to allow Joseph to go with them against his better judgment. He simply sends Joseph to find them. In fact, there is no dialogue between the brothers and Jacob until after Joseph has been disposed of, and even then they do not encounter their father face to face, but have the robe sent to him (v. 32). This is a particularly interesting difference from the Qurʾan's account, where the brothers actually tell their father what the bloody shirt means: "Oh our father, we hastily went off leaving Joseph with our provisions and a wolf devoured him!" In the Bible the brothers avoid any direct contact with Jacob and simply send the bloody evidence to him, thereby forcing him to interpret its meaning and reach the wrong conclusion. Technically they have not lied to their father as they do in the Islamic text. The only words they say to him in Genesis are found in v. 32, and nothing about them is patently false. "This we have found; see now whether it is your son's robe or not."

The brothers in Genesis do not come across as the lying, conniving bunch that they are in the Qur'an, but they are just as duplicitous and guilty. They are forced to realize their goal by different means in Genesis because of the important role knowledge, or lack of it, plays in the biblical story. The key question surrounds the fate of Joseph in the well. What do the brothers know and when do they know it? In the Qur'an one of them advises the others not to kill Joseph but to cast him in a well where some travelers will come upon him. After agreeing to this plan they go to their father and persuade him to allow Joseph to accompany them. When they toss him into the well they assume travelers will rescue him, and this is precisely what happens. Things go more or less according to plan for them, and they are able to return confidently to their father and tell him the concocted lie about the wolf.

The biblical brothers lack this certainty. Reuben comes up with the idea of throwing Joseph into a pit, but the narrator alerts the reader that Reuben actually intends to rescue his brother and bring him back to Jacob (v. 22). The brothers then sit down for a meal and devise a plan to sell Joseph to a caravan of Ishmaelites. Before this can happen, Midianite travelers happen upon Joseph and sell him to the Ishmaelites. When Reuben returns to the pit to rescue Joseph he is stunned to find that he is no longer there (vv. 25-30). Joseph has vanished into thin air and the brothers do not know what has happened to him!

Their lack of knowledge about Joseph's whereabouts is why the brothers go on to act the way they do in Genesis. For all they know, Joseph may have escaped or has been rescued from the well and is now on his way back home to tell Jacob what his brothers did to him. This explains their reluctance to confront Jacob personally with the bad news of Joseph's tragic death. A safer strategy is to keep their distance, send the bloodied robe home, and see what reaction it elicits from their father. If, like their counterparts in the Qur'an, they tell Jacob that Joseph is dead and he suddenly shows up, the brothers will have much explaining to do. But if their father reaches this conclusion on his own they will be less culpable and will have an easier time defending their actions. Their relative tentativeness and lack of manipulation in Genesis, then, is a function of their lack of knowledge regarding Joseph's status.

The central role that lack of knowledge plays in the biblical passage is something that might be easily overlooked by the reader who gets caught up in the drama and tension in the Genesis story. But the high profile of the theme in the Qur'an where knowledge, whether actual or imagined, informs the thoughts of all the characters helps to bring this aspect of the biblical narrative to the surface. When we reread the Genesis text from this perspective we note that here, too, knowledge is a major motif in the telling. Every character in Genesis is in the dark. Jacob knows nothing and reaches the wrong conclusions about what he thinks he knows. Joseph knows nothing, and the lack of a divine message of comfort makes him even more ignorant of his circumstances. The brothers in the Bible are not the know-it-alls they are in the Qur'an, and their lack of knowledge about Joseph's fate causes them to be circumspect in their dealings with their father.

Perhaps the question that looms largest in the biblical story when we read it in light of the Qur'an version concerns the divine character. What does God know? In the Islamic text Allah speaks to Joseph and is invoked by Jacob, and therefore has a role in the passage. In this first section of the Joseph story in Genesis, God has not yet been mentioned or made an appearance. The Qur'an text ends with the reassuring words that Allah is aware of what has been done, but the Bible reader must wait to discover the extent of the deity's involvement in the lives of Joseph and his family.

CHAPTER TWO

The Narrator and Characters:
Joseph and Potiphar's Wife
(Genesis 39:1-19; Qur'an 12:21-34)

The Bible and the Qur'an both report that Joseph is rescued from the well by a group of travelers and ends up in Egypt where he becomes part of the household of a man whose wife unsuccessfully attempts to seduce him. This is one of the most famous scenes of the entire Joseph story, and it has been the subject of countless works of art in Judaism, Christianity, and Islam. It is a well-written narrative of sexual intrigue that addresses issues like unfulfilled desire, revenge, and moral responsibility, themes that have spoken to people for ages.

Our analysis of this section is mainly interested in how the information contained in the story is communicated to the reader. What role does the narrator play? Does the reader learn about the characters through their own words and actions, or through some other means? How is time presented and manipulated in the text? Attention to these and related issues can teach us a great deal about how a text is constructed and how it attempts to persuade its readers to accept its version of the events.

The attempted seduction is the focal point of the narrative for both the Qur'an and the Bible. But before describing that encounter each text presents some background information that exerts influence on how the reader will evaluate the characters. We will examine these two sections separately, but first some comments on how stories are organized and structured are in order.

The Greek philosopher Aristotle was the first person to engage in critical study of literary works, and he determined that plots are composed of three parts: a beginning, a middle, and an end. The beginning, or exposition, presents the background information of the story that helps to establish the context of the narrative for the reader. The end is the conclusion of the story describing the situation after the events of the narrative have taken place. The middle section is where most of the action of the plot usually occurs. This section is typically divided into three subsections. The first is the complication that introduces some element into the story that will lead to a crisis for one or more of the characters. The second is the change that is brought about as a result of this complication. This can be an external change of situation in which the circumstances of the character(s) have been altered in some way, or it can be an internal change of knowledge whereby the character(s) now know(s) something previously unknown. The third subsection is the resolution or unraveling, in which the results of the change are made apparent to the reader.

It is common to speak of a book or a story as having a single plot, but if we apply this framework to most narratives it is apparent that, in fact, they usually contain a number of sequential or interrelated plots. This will become clear when we think of the first section of the Joseph story that was treated in the previous chapter. Within the context of the Joseph story as a whole it functions as the exposition, since it introduces some of the major characters and explains how Joseph ends up in Egypt, where most of the remainder of the narrative will take place. But if we think of it as an independent unit it is an entire plot unto itself, since it has its own complication, change, and resolution.

In addition, we can often identify more than one of each of these elements in a given story. For example, where do we locate the change in Genesis 37? Joseph goes through a significant change of situation when his brothers throw him into the well. But Jacob also experiences a change of knowledge when he receives the false word that Joseph has been killed. While the change Joseph undergoes might be more significant in terms of the overall story of Genesis 37–50, that of Jacob also plays an important role as the narrative unfolds. We should therefore keep in mind that narratives like the Joseph story are often composed of discrete subunits that contribute to the overall organization of the larger plot but can also be studied as separate literary entities in their own right. The structure of the section we now turn to is a case in point.

Prelude to a Kiss (Genesis 39:1-6; Qur'an 12:21-22)

As noted above, before describing the attempted seduction the Bible and the Qur'an provide the reader with some background information. In the biblical text this material is found in Genesis 39:1-6.

> ¹Now Joseph was taken down to Egypt, and Potiphar, an officer of Pharaoh, the captain of the guard, an Egyptian, bought him from the

Ishmaelites who had brought him down there. ²The Lord was with Joseph, and he became a successful man; he was in the house of his Egyptian master. ³His master saw that the Lord was with him, and that the Lord caused all that he did to prosper in his hands. ⁴So Joseph found favor in his sight and attended him; he made him overseer of his house and put him in charge of all that he had. ⁵From the time that he made him overseer in his house and over all that he had, the Lord blessed the Egyptian's house for Joseph's sake; the blessing of the Lord was on all that he had, in house and field. ⁶So he left all that he had in Joseph's charge; and, with him there, he had no concern for anything but the food that he ate. Now Joseph was handsome and good-looking.

Taken on their own, these six verses are an independent narrative unit since they tell a story and contain the basic elements of a plot. They describe Joseph's arrival in Egypt, his entry into his master's house, and the subsequent success he and his master both enjoy as a result of his presence there. Viewed in a broader context these verses also function as the exposition or first part of the story that follows, recounting the attempted seduction by Potiphar's wife. They explain how Joseph found himself in a position of authority and trust that would enable him to be alone with the woman.

The reference to Joseph's good looks in the last sentence of the section makes the connection with the following story particularly clear. Biblical narrative rarely comments on the physical features of characters, but when it does so those physical qualities usually play an important role in the story. In this case mention that Joseph is handsome helps to explain why his master's wife is attracted to him. An interesting feature of this section is that it comes entirely from the narrator. With rare exceptions, in biblical literature the narrator is always an omniscient, third-person voice who is not a character in the story. To say that the narrator is omniscient is not to say that the narrator reports everything. Certain things are reported, but others are left unexpressed, and it is the author who determines what the narrator divulges and what is left out. As we will see, the choice is a critical one because it has a significant effect on the reader's experience of the text. In the Bible the narrator's voice is always a reliable one that can be trusted and accepted as true. If the narrator does not provide information, or if the reader gains knowledge from another less reliable source, this leads to gaps and ambiguities in the text that can raise questions in the reader's mind. These issues will be treated in later chapters.

The method of characterization used in a text is a significant component that is easy to overlook. If the reader is told something about a character, this is called direct characterization. When it comes from the biblical narrator the reader should accept the information as accurate and correct. But when it comes from somewhere else, such as another character, the reader must exercise caution since, for a variety of reasons, characters do not always speak the truth. This difference can be illustrated by comparing two verses in Genesis 37. Jacob's words in v. 33 of that chapter are an example of direct characterization by another character. "A wild animal has devoured him; Joseph is without doubt torn to pieces." Jacob's characterization of Joseph as dead is erroneous because his other sons have deceived him into thinking this is so. But when the narrator describes Joseph's fate five verses earlier there is no doubt in the reader's mind that this is precisely what has happened to him. "When some Midianite traders passed by, they drew Joseph up, lifting him out of the pit, and sold him to the Ishmaelites for twenty pieces of silver. And they took Joseph to Egypt."

Another method commonly employed in narrative is indirect characterization. Here the reader is not given direct, explicit information about a character but instead attempts to form an impression about that character through a consideration of his or her actions and words in the narrative. This often leads to ambiguous and unclear conclusions. A character's behavior and speech can be hard to interpret because the reader is not always privy to his or her motivations and thoughts. Occasionally, though, more certainty is possible. For example, sometimes the conclusions one draws from indirect characterization can be verified by what is reliably known through direct characterization on the part of the narrator.

Returning to Genesis 37, we can see this principle in operation. In v. 22 Reuben attempts to dissuade his brothers from killing Joseph by offering them another option. "Shed no blood; throw him into this pit here in the wilderness, but lay no hand on him." These words shed indirect light on Reuben's character, but the reader has no way of knowing precisely what they say about him. What is his motivation for trying to spare Joseph? Do his words suggest the reader should evaluate his character positively, or does he have some sinister alternative plan for his brother? The narrator's direct characterization follows immediately in the second half of the verse and suggests the reader should adopt a more positive view of Reuben because he said this "that he might rescue him out of their hand and restore him to their father."

Because Gen 39:1-6 comes from the narrator, the reader accepts the information it contains as reliable and trustworthy. The narrator directly characterizes Joseph and his master, and there is no reason to doubt what is learned: Joseph became successful and his success rubbed off on his master. The narrator also explains the reason for their success and introduces a theological element into the text. Joseph and his master have prospered because the Lord is with Joseph. This point is made through the use of repetition, a standard literary device often found in the Bible that will be discussed in detail in a later chapter. In order to call attention to some aspect of a story or to stress its importance, biblical writers often repeat it throughout the course of a text. In these six verses "the Lord" is mentioned five times, which is a high concentration of a term in a relatively brief section. The reader discovers that God is with Joseph (v. 2), his master knows God is with him (v. 3), God is the cause of Joseph's success (v. 3), and God has blessed the Egyptian's house and possessions (v. 5). Because the narrator is the source of this information it is accepted as accurate and true.

The theological focus of this section is in marked contrast to what was seen in ch. 37, where God is never mentioned. When Joseph is abandoned in the well by his brothers, the reader wonders where God is. But upon his arrival in Egypt the matter is not in doubt since the reader learns immediately that the Lord is actively present in his life. This information would not be as readily accepted if it had come from some other source, such as another character in the narrative.

As mentioned above, the narrator is omniscient but does not reveal everything. In these verses the reader learns that the Lord is with Joseph and that Potiphar recognizes it, but is left in the dark about another matter of some importance. Does Joseph know the Lord is with him? The narrator never says this explicitly, so the reader is left to wonder about Joseph's character and the extent of his knowledge. The question of Joseph's knowledge of God is an issue that we will be tracking regularly, particularly when we engage in comparative study of the Genesis and Qurʾan texts.

A final aspect of the biblical text to consider before turning to its parallel in the Qurʾan is its use of time. In literary study a distinction is often made between narrated time and narration time. Put simply, narrated time is the amount of time that passes in the world of a story, while narration time is the amount of time it takes to read the story. This can be illustrated by considering the episode in Gen 37:15-17 in which Joseph encounters the man who tells him his brothers left Shechem and went to Dothan. The end of that text says: "So Joseph went after his brothers and found them at Dothan." Dothan is about ten miles from Shechem and, under the best of circumstances, it would take some three to four hours to cover that distance. This is the narrated time of the text. But the duration of Joseph's journey is treated in a mere eleven words, only six in the original Hebrew text. The narration time, the time it takes to read those words, is only a few seconds.

Narrative time and narrated time often differ considerably, due to the use of expressions such as "after a while" and "the next week" that compress extended periods of time. Similarly, a lengthy physical description of a scene can sometimes stretch on for a longer period of time than the events that are being narrated. The two are closest when dialogue is reported, since it takes the reader about the same amount of time to read the words as it does for the character to say them. The author's manipulation of time in a narrative can sometimes have a dramatic effect on how the reader experiences a story.

There are no chronological indicators in Gen 39:1-6, so it is very difficult for the reader to determine how much time passes between v. 1 and v. 6. The only thing that can be said with certainty is that the narrated time is longer than narration time. But we have no way of knowing things like how long it took for Joseph to arrive in Egypt or for Potiphar to see that the Lord was with him. The only clue the text provides that suggests it covers a fairly lengthy period of time is the reference to the master's field being blessed in v. 5, indicating the completion of at least one agricultural season. This lack of attention to matters of time is probably due to the function of this section of the story. Because it is the exposition to the "main event," the attempted seduction, the author is primarily interested in setting the context for what will happen by giving the reader the information necessary to understand the scene that is about to be related. Relatively insignificant matters like time indicators that do not serve that purpose are therefore irrelevant and unnecessary.

As is often the case, the Qur'an's parallel to this material is briefer, covering in only two verses what Genesis describes in six.

> [21]The Egyptian who bought him said to his wife, "Treat him well during his lodging. Perhaps he will be of benefit to us and we will take him as a son." Thus did We establish Joseph in the land and We taught him the interpretation of events. Allah controlled his affairs although most people do not know. [22]When he reached maturity We gave him wisdom and knowledge. Thus do We reward those who are good.

Unlike its counterpart in Genesis, this text does not come entirely from the narrator. Joseph's master speaks in v. 21, and his words provide some important information. First of all, the reader learns at the outset that the man is married, a fact that is not revealed until the seventh verse of the section in the Bible. This information is withheld in Genesis in order to realize a certain dramatic effect. The news that Potiphar has a wife is delayed until after the mention of Joseph's good looks, and she is introduced in a way that causes the reader to suspect trouble is around the corner. "Now Joseph was handsome and good-looking. And after a time his master's wife cast her eyes on Joseph." The reader's suspicions are confirmed by the very next words in the text: "And (she) said, 'Lie with me.'"

In its own way the Qur'an text also anticipates the attempted seduction, only in a more subtle fashion. The master's request that his wife treat Joseph well during his stay with them raises a question in the reader's mind about her character (why would she need to be told this?), and it prefigures future events when she will not follow this advice, but will mistreat Joseph.

Another interesting piece of information that is disclosed by the master's words concerns Joseph's age at this point in the narrative. He entertains the possibility that he and his wife might take Joseph as a son, thereby indicating that Joseph is probably a bit younger than his seventeen-year-old biblical counterpart (Gen 37:2). This might also suggest that the wife is significantly older than Joseph, an element that adds a twist to the upcoming seduction scene.

Except for this one line of dialogue from the master, it is the narrator who speaks throughout these two verses in the Qur'an. But the source of that narratorial voice differs significantly in the two texts. Whereas the biblical narrator is anonymous and unknown, the identity of the narrator of Islam's scripture is never in doubt. This is the voice of Allah, who, according to Muslim belief, communicated the contents of the book directly to the prophet Muhammad through the agency of the angel Gabriel. This means that the narrator of the Qur'an enjoys a position of privilege that is unavailable to the biblical one. The distinction between deity and narrator typical of the Bible is not found in the Islamic text, where the two are identical. There is therefore a theological reason why the reader of the Qur'an should accept the narrator's voice as omniscient and reliable.

As was the case with the Genesis account, it is difficult to get an accurate sense of the narrated time of this passage. Verse 22 makes reference to Allah's gift of wisdom and knowledge to Joseph "when he reached maturity," but when exactly was this in relation to the point at which the Egyptian brought him into his house? Similarly, it is unclear whether the expressions of divine favor directed toward Joseph should be understood as occurring sequentially over a period of time or if he received them all at once. In other words, did Allah establish Joseph, teach him, control his affairs, and give him wisdom and knowledge all at once, or did these things occur over time? Once again this lack of concern for precise chronology can be explained by recognizing the function these verses serve in the larger narrative. Like the biblical version, the Qur'an is primarily interested in providing the reader with the information necessary to properly interpret and understand the upcoming seduction scene. Anything not serving that purpose is unnecessary.

Here, as in Genesis, that background information is mostly theological in nature. The text goes to significant lengths to explain all Allah has done for Joseph: his position in the land, his ability to interpret events, his well-controlled affairs, and his wisdom and knowledge are all the result of divine largesse. The reference to interpretation of events is noteworthy because this same phrase is found on Jacob's lips in v. 6 of the Qurʾan passage. After he advises Joseph not to tell his brothers of his vision Jacob predicts what Allah will do for Joseph in the future; this includes teaching him how to interpret events. The words in the Arabic text are identical in the two verses, and so the reader hears from the divine narrator that the very thing Jacob envisioned has come to pass. This validates the close relationship with the deity that Jacob appeared to have in the previous section of the Qurʾan story and establishes him as a credible character in the reader's mind. This is another example of how repetition can function as a literary device that influences the reading experience.

A key difference between the Genesis and Qurʾan versions is found in the last sentence of v. 21: "Allah controlled his affairs although most people do not know." This statement asserts that the majority of people are unaware of the role that Allah plays in Joseph's life, a situation unlike that found in Gen 39:1-6. We noted that in the biblical narrative his master, in particular, is conscious of what God has done for Joseph, and that this is the main reason why the Egyptian is able to prosper. Whereas the Qurʾan text calls attention to people's ignorance about Joseph's relationship with God, the Genesis story highlights the fact that it is known and recognized by others. This is an important aspect of the narratives that will be discussed in several places in the coming chapters.

Our comparison of how the two texts present the introductory material before the attempted seduction sheds light on their agendas. We learn a great deal about Joseph in both books and much of that knowledge is theological in nature since each version calls attention to what God has done for him. In fact, the Qurʾan focuses almost entirely on Joseph's relationship with the deity. The only reference to Joseph in relation to other human characters is found in the first half of v. 21 when the master instructs his wife to treat Joseph well and suggests that they might take him as a son. But there is no description of Joseph interacting with or speaking with them or any other person. The rest of the section deals exclusively with Joseph's relationship with Allah.

The Genesis account, on the other hand, puts more emphasis on the relationship between Joseph and Potiphar. It adopts the opposite order of the Qurʾan and presents first the fact that the Lord is with Joseph (39:2a). It then offers a fairly lengthy description of the effect this has on Joseph's relationship with his master (39:2a-6a). Joseph's presence in his master's house, the favor he finds in his sight, his position as overseer, and the trust he inspires in his master are all elements of the Bible's telling of the story that are not present in the Qur'an. They give the reader a fairly detailed picture of the relationship that exists between Joseph and Potiphar that is unavailable to the reader of the Qur'an.

At this point in the narrative the Joseph of the Qur'an has a more developed relationship with God than his biblical counterpart does. This is something that will be apparent in the seduction scene and elsewhere throughout the story. The foundation of that relationship is presented here in clear and exact language: Allah establishes him in the land, teaches him the interpretation of events, controls his affairs, and rewards him with wisdom and knowledge. The only thing the Genesis reader knows is that the Lord is "with Joseph," a phrase that indicates divine presence but lacks any specificity. In fact, the same might be said about Potiphar: The Lord is also "with him" since his house and possessions have been blessed. The Islamic text, on the other hand, sets Joseph apart from others by calling attention to what is distinct in his relationship with Allah.

The Qur'an's emphasis on Allah's role as guide and protector for Joseph is perhaps best seen in the divine gifts of wisdom and knowledge he receives. In the previous chapter we noted that true wisdom and knowledge reside only with Allah. In v. 6 Jacob refers to Allah as "the one who knows, the wise one." The deity is now equipping Joseph with the tools necessary to live a good and proper life. Interestingly, the Bible also calls attention to two traits Joseph possesses, but this time they are physical qualities: he is handsome and good-looking. These, too, may have their source in God, but they do not prepare Joseph as well for the challenges he will face. In fact, they appear to be an obstacle to his living a good and proper life. His wisdom and knowledge will allow him to overcome the advances of his master's wife in the Qur'an, but his physical attributes are the reason why she attempts to seduce him in Genesis.

She Said, He Said (Genesis 39:7-19; Qur'an 12:23-29)

The scene of the attempted seduction offers an excellent opportunity to explore the area of characterization. The Bible and the Qur'an both present it as an episode full of dramatic tension in which the characters are richly drawn, and the reader is inevitably drawn into their world as the story unfolds. The Qur'an's version is found in 12:23-29.

> [23]But the woman in whose house he was living tried to entice him. She locked the doors and said, "Come here." He responded, "Allah forbid! My master has made well my lodging. Evildoers do not prosper." [24]She desired him and he would have desired her if not for the clear proof of

his Lord. Thus, We turned back evil and immorality from him. Truly, he is one of Our sincere servants. [25]They ran to the door and she ripped his shirt from behind. They met her husband at the door. She said, "There is no penalty for a man who desires to do evil to your family other than imprisonment or painful punishment." [26]He responded, "She tried to entice me!" A witness from her family testified, "If his shirt is torn in the front, she is telling the truth and he is a liar. [27]But if his shirt is torn from behind, then she is lying and he is truthful." [28]When he saw that his shirt was torn from behind he said, "This is one of your plots. Truly, your plots are great. [29]Ignore this, Joseph. You, woman, ask forgiveness for your offense. Truly, you are a sinner."

Obviously the wife does not follow the advice her husband gave her in v. 21 when he urged her to treat Joseph well during his stay with them. She does just the opposite by first trying to lure him into an inappropriate sexual relationship and then placing the blame on Joseph when her husband unexpectedly arrives on the scene. The intensity of her attraction to Joseph is reflected in her actions. She locks the doors to the room they are in and runs after him when he tries to escape, ripping the shirt off his back in the process. The narrator affirms this impression of the wife by directly characterizing her as "desiring him" (v. 24).

When she locks the doors the wife expresses a degree of premeditation that indicates the attempted seduction is not a spur-of-the-moment show of passion. But the motivation behind the act is ambiguous. Does she lock the doors because she does not want someone to barge into the room and find them in a compromising situation? Does she lock them because she wants to prevent Joseph from fleeing her presence? Or does she lock them because both of these scenarios are possible in her mind? If these questions could be answered with certainty it would result in an indirect characterization of Joseph on her part that would give the reader a sense of what she thinks of his character. If she locked the doors to prevent someone on the outside from intruding, it would suggest she thinks that Joseph will be a willing partner in the affair. On the other hand, if she locked the doors to keep him in, she probably believes he is not going to cooperate and will need to be coerced. The ambiguity cannot be resolved, but, as is usually the case, it adds an intriguing dimension to the wife's character that complicates the reader's evaluation of her.

If the doors had not been locked Joseph would have been long gone. The Qur'an paints him as a character who is above reproach and able to withstand the temptation of his master's wife. His words tell us as much. "Allah forbid! My master has made well my lodging. Evildoers do not prosper." His act of running to the door is in keeping with the message of his words. In addition to the testimony of Joseph himself, the narrator weighs in with some direct characterization that continues the theme begun in vv. 21b and 22 when the narratorial voice was first heard. "She desired him and he would have desired her if not for the clear proof of his Lord. Thus, We turned back evil and immorality from him. Truly, he is one of Our sincere servants."

These words call attention both to Joseph's special relationship with Allah and to his humanity. Ultimately it is Allah who makes Joseph a good and moral person. This may be an oblique reference to the wisdom and knowledge the deity has given him (v. 22), enabling him to fend off the advances of his master's wife. The comment that Joseph would have otherwise desired her is an explicit recognition of his human nature. According to Islamic belief all human beings, including prophets like Joseph, are susceptible to temptation and have the capacity to sin. The mercy and grace of Allah, along with a desire to follow the divine will, are what enable one to stay on the straight path. Those who do so are worthy of the title bestowed on Joseph: "one of Our sincere servants."

This is an interesting title in light of the content of the narrative. The story recounts Joseph's experiences as a servant in the Egyptian's house, but the narrator reminds the reader that this is not the true nature of Joseph's servanthood. He is first and foremost a servant of Allah, the only true master. This, in turn, introduces a degree of ambiguity into Joseph's words. When he deflects the woman's come-on with the comment that his master has made well his lodging, which master does Joseph have in mind?

Several clues in the text suggest that Joseph is speaking of Allah when he refers to his master in v. 23. First of all, the comment is preceded by the exclamation "Allah forbid!" The reference to "my master" immediately after this could be an example of apposition, a grammatical term that refers to the use of two different words or titles to refer to the same individual. In the present case Joseph may be making use of apposition by identifying the deity as both "Allah" and "my master." Another clue can be seen in Allah's designation of Joseph as "one of Our servants" in v. 24. This may be a way of picking up on the theme that Joseph has introduced and stating that Allah is, in fact, the master of whom he speaks in v. 23.

Yet another argument for seeing Allah as Joseph's master in v. 23 is one that is based on linguistic and contextual grounds. When Joseph says that his master has "made well my lodging" his words recall the Egyptian's request to his wife that she "treat him (Joseph) well during his lodging" in v. 21. In fact, the Arabic term "lodging" *(matwā)* is identical in both. In the intervening v. 22 the narrator tells the reader that Allah, not his human master, is the one who has established Joseph in the land and controlled his affairs. Joseph, too, is aware of this since he possesses wisdom and knowledge given to him by Allah. It is therefore logical to conclude that the master he mentions in v. 23 can only be Allah, who has truly made well his lodging.

This conclusion is further supported by the fact that when Allah is referred to as Joseph's Lord earlier in v. 24 the Arabic term that is used *(rabb)* is the same one that is translated as "master" in v. 23. In fact, in the entire Qur'an story the Egyptian in whose house he is living is never called Joseph's *rabb*. Only Allah is given this title in relation to Joseph, and this argues in favor of understanding it this way in v. 23 as well.

Even if Joseph is speaking of Allah as his master, this may not be what the wife is hearing. The text does not indicate that she is aware of the information the narrator has just imparted to the reader, so she may be totally ignorant of the relationship Joseph has with Allah. She may be assuming that he is referring to her husband, and so it would be a mistake to interpret her persistence in going after Joseph as somehow a rejection of his faith in Allah. Once again, the ambiguity that pervades the scene complicates how the reader should interpret it.

A final aspect of Joseph's character that deserves brief comment is the fact that he attempts to defend himself after he is falsely accused. His denial of any wrongdoing in v. 26 reflects his sense of justice and relates back to his remark to the woman in v. 23 that evildoers do not prosper. If he does not speak up now she will be off the hook, and that principle will have been violated. His claim of innocence is also a key element in the narrative, because without it the witness might not have stepped forward and suggested the test that absolved Joseph of guilt.

The husband does not play a very prominent role in the seduction scene, but his character is used to great effect. His arrival just at the moment they race to the door is a dramatic high point that leaves the reader guessing what his response will be. But the man does not speak. He will not utter a word until every other character in the story says something. His wife goes first and, displaying an impressive ability to think on her feet, shifts the blame to Joseph. This leads to Joseph's profession of innocence, setting up a classic case of "she said, he said." The reader continues to wonder what the husband will do.

Before that question can be answered, the witness comes forward and proposes a way of getting at the truth. Only at this point does the husband speak and reveal his reaction to the circumstances. Delaying the husband's response by having the other characters speak first is a very effective technique that prolongs the narrative and pulls the reader into the world of the story. It resolves the complication of the plot in a more memorable and satisfying way than if the man had observed the torn shirt on his own and immediately rendered his verdict.

A couple of things about the husband's response are noteworthy. First of all, the double reference to plots in v. 28 makes use of the same Arabic root *(kāda)* found twice in v. 5 when Jacob warned Joseph about the potential plotting of his brothers. The resumption of that theme here contributes to the image of Joseph as an innocent victim who needs to be cautious not only in his relationship with his brothers but with others who might wish to harm him.

When the husband speaks of "your plots" in this verse he is not only referring to his wife's plots, because the word "your" is in the feminine plural form. In effect he is saying that the plots of "you women" are great. This is an odd construction that, as we will see, is best understood in light of the Qurʾan scene that follows and will be treated below.

The other striking aspect of the husband's comments in v. 29 is that they are loaded with theological language. The Arabic words translated here as "ask forgiveness" *(istaġfara),* "offense" *(ḏanb),* and "sinner" *(ḫāṭiʾ)* are all terms primarily used to describe violations of the divine will and the means by which one can overcome them in order to regain a proper relationship with God. This is an interesting element of the Egyptian's character because it indicates that he interprets his wife's actions as not only harmful to Joseph but somehow directed against Allah. In other words, he appears to be a man of faith who is concerned with the theological consequences of what she has done and is not simply thinking of the social ramifications.

The setting of a story is an important element that often helps to create a mood and shape the reading experience. In the seduction scene in the Qurʾan the setting conveys a feeling of confinement that highlights Joseph's precarious situation and enables the reader to identify with him. The precise location of the scene is not given, but a sense of the enclosed space in which it occurs is conveyed through the triple mention of the door(s). Symbolically, the door represents a border that Joseph is not allowed to cross. When the woman locks it and makes his passage impossible, Joseph becomes a prisoner in her world, unable to escape. This sense of entrapment is heightened when he rushes to the door only to meet her husband, who is yet another potential barrier to his freedom.

No other details are provided for the setting. Where are they in the house? What is in the room? Which door do they run to? What time of day is it? Only the doors are mentioned, but they have a tremendous impact on the story. In fact, the lack of reference to other aspects of the setting makes the doors all the more prominent. They are the focus of attention and are the dominant architectural and physical feature of the scene as the reader envisions it. Joseph is trapped in an enclosed space behind locked doors and cannot escape.

The Bible's description of the encounter between Joseph and Potiphar's wife is found in Gen 39:7-19:

> [7]And after a time his master's wife cast her eyes on Joseph and said, "Lie with me." [8]But he refused and said to his master's wife, "Look, with me here, my master has no concern about anything in the house, and he has put everything that he has in my hand. [9]He is not greater in this house than I am, nor has he kept back anything from me except yourself, because you are his wife. How then could I do this great wickedness, and sin against God?" [10]And although she spoke to Joseph day after day, he would not consent to lie beside her or to be with her. [11]One day, however, when he went into the house to do his work, and while no one else was in the house, [12]she caught hold of his garment, saying, "Lie with me!" But he left his garment in her hand, and fled and ran outside. [13]When she saw that he had left his garment in her hand and had fled outside, [14]she called out to the members of her household and said to them, "See, my husband has brought among us a Hebrew to insult us! He came in to me to lie with me, and I cried out with a loud voice; [15]and when he heard me raise my voice and cry out, he left his garment beside me, and fled outside." [16]Then she kept his garment by her until his master came home, [17]and she told him the same story, saying, "The Hebrew servant, whom you have brought among us, came in to me to insult me; [18]but as soon as I raised my voice and cried out, he left his garment beside me, and fled outside." [19]When his master heard the words that his wife spoke to him, saying, "This is the way your servant treated me," he became enraged.

We have seen that when the wife locks the doors in the Qurʾan it is an action that reflects a certain level of premeditation on her part. This aspect of her character is expanded in Genesis, where she is presented as a calculating woman who knows what she wants and will go to any lengths to get it. As far as the reader knows, the attempted seduction in the Islamic text is an isolated incident that could be the result of a moment of weakness when she finds herself in the rare situation of being alone with Joseph. This is not the case in the Bible since she continues to work on Joseph "day after day" (v. 10) despite the rebuff she receives after the first attempt. The events of the climactic scene that finds them together are the culmination of a prolonged and sustained effort on the woman's part to win over Joseph and not simply due to coincidence or the heat of the moment.

Her premeditation in Genesis extends beyond the attempted seduction. After Joseph flees and leaves her holding his clothing she has some time to think about what her next move will be. They have not been caught red-handed by her husband as in the Qurʾan, and so she has the option to keep silent and let the matter drop. But she chooses not to follow this course. She keeps the garment and recruits members of her household as unwitting accomplices in the scheme she devises. Therefore her premeditation in Genesis is a factor not just in her attempts to entice Joseph but also in her response when he rebukes her efforts. A quality that is presented in a subtle and ambiguous way in the Qurʾan is her defining trait in the Bible.

The time element is interesting in relation to the woman's premeditation. According to v. 26 she kept Joseph's garment by her "until his master came home." The reader has no way of knowing the narrated time involved in this statement. Did her husband come back later that day, or was he on an extended trip and did not return until much later? If the latter is the case, her inability to drop the matter would reflect the depth of her anger at Joseph and her desire for revenge. The question must remain unresolved since it is impossible to know how long she waited. But here is an example of how attention to the use of time in a narrative can have an impact on how the reader perceives a character.

The negative assessment of her character that the reader has begun to formulate is affirmed as the narrative unfolds. Feigning indignation, she implicates her husband and claims he is partially responsible for the humiliation she has had to endure. First she attempts to garner sympathy from the members of her household: "See, my husband has brought among us a Hebrew to insult us!" Then, when he returns home, she points an accusatory finger directly at her husband. "The Hebrew servant, whom you have brought among us, came in to me to insult me." In both places she calls attention to Joseph's Hebrew ancestry, thereby adding insult to injury by underscoring the fact that the man who has offended her is a foreigner. She also points to her husband's culpability in both lines by stating that he is the one responsible for bringing Joseph into the house in the first place.

A comparative analysis of how the wife is presented in the Bible and the Qurʾan leads to interesting results. In both cases she attempts to seduce Joseph and deceive her husband, but the wife of the Qurʾan fares better in the mind of the reader. In a sense she can be viewed as a victim of circumstances in the Islamic text. She gives in to her desire when she finds herself in the presence of a man she is attracted to, and is forced to lie to her husband when he arrives on the scene unexpectedly. She is a tragic and pathetic figure, literally chasing after the object of her affection and making up a story on the spot to avoid further embarrassment.

This is not the impression the Bible reader has of her. The wife in Genesis is a manipulative and vindictive person. Her attraction to Joseph borders on the obsessive and she refuses to take no for an answer. Unlike her Islamic counterpart who is caught in the act, she has time to think about her situation and is not forced to concoct a story on the fly. The woman in the Bible accuses Joseph because she has been spurned, not because she has been discovered. She also gets away with it. When the wife's lie is exposed in the Qur'an her husband asks her to admit her mistake and begin the process of rehabilitation. But when the biblical wife gets off scot-free the reader can only wonder what, or who, will catch her eye next time.

The heavy emphasis the Qur'an's version of the attempted seduction places on Joseph's relationship with Allah has already been noted. The narrator informs us that the deity is the primary reason why Joseph is able to fend off the woman's advances (v. 24), and Joseph himself appears to refer to Allah in v. 23 when he says his master has made well his lodging. In Genesis, on the other hand, Joseph's relationship with Potiphar, his earthly master, is the focus of attention. This is in keeping with the difference already observed regarding how the background material to the seduction is presented in the two books. In the Islamic text (vv. 21-22) Allah's presence in Joseph's life is the dominant theme. In Genesis (39:1-6), on the other hand, Joseph's relationship with God is presented within the context of his relationship with Potiphar.

Is the biblical Joseph able to avoid giving in to the woman because he receives God's assistance? The answer to that question is not as clear as in the Qur'an where Allah (the narrator) bluntly states that this is the case. In Genesis, God never explicitly claims to be the source of Joseph's resolve, and so the reader is left to wonder what role, if any, the deity plays in the scene. One might appeal to the opening verses of ch. 39 where it is stated that the Lord is with Joseph and then argue that the same is true in this scene, where the Lord continues to be with him as he is tempted by his master's wife. But this is to read between the lines in a way that is unnecessary in the Qur'an. A further argument against this approach is the fact that the background material in Gen 39:1-6 speaks only of the physical and tangible benefits Joseph receives from his Lord being with him, and does not mention how his moral character or disposition are affected by God's presence. There is, then, an ambiguity about the deity's relationship to Joseph in the biblical scene that is not found in the Qur'an.

This is not to say that the Genesis text is completely lacking theological content. In v. 9 Joseph interprets an affair with the woman as a "sin against God." But this acknowledgement only comes at the end of a fairly lengthy response to her invitation that is centered on his relationship with

Potiphar, not God. Joseph reminds her of the terms of the agreement between himself and her husband: his master has no concerns because he has placed everything in Joseph's hands. He then goes so far as to claim equality with Potiphar—"he is not greater in this house than I am"—except where his wife is concerned. Only after describing these ground rules does Joseph introduce a theological element and speak of a possible sin.

The difference between the two texts on this point is striking. The Qur'an's Joseph begins his refusal with the exclamation "Allah forbid!" and then he and the narrator focus on all that the deity has done for him. The theological consequences of the potential act are clearly to the fore: if Joseph sleeps with the woman his relationship with Allah will be damaged. The relationship he has with the woman's husband is not mentioned and never enters the picture. But in *his* response the Joseph of Genesis chooses to begin with and concentrate on his ties to Potiphar. He eventually gets around to mentioning that this would also be an offense to God, but when compared to his words in the Qur'an this comment almost sounds like an afterthought. It appears that his relationship with Potiphar is primary in the eyes of the biblical Joseph, and this lends his character an air of ambition, even selfishness, that his Islamic counterpart lacks. If the Joseph of the Qur'an gives in to her wishes he might lose his soul. If the Joseph in Genesis does, he might lose his job.

This impression is reinforced by a consideration of the vocabulary employed by the Genesis version. We have noted that the Qur'an leaves no doubt that Allah is Joseph's true master. In the Bible it is Potiphar who holds that title, as evidenced by the fact that the term "master" occurs five times (vv. 7, 8 [twice], 16, 19), all referring to the Egyptian. In each of those cases Potiphar is called either "his master" or "my master," underscoring the relational dimension of the term and defining Joseph's true identity. Although the husband is identified as Potiphar twice elsewhere in the biblical text (37:36; 39:1), his personal name is avoided here in favor of the title that asserts his authority over Joseph. A similar technique that makes the same point is employed with regard to Joseph when he is referred to in rapid succession as a "Hebrew" (v. 14), "the Hebrew servant" (v. 17), and "your servant" (v. 19).

Joseph is a servant in both texts, but he owes his allegiance to a different master in each. This has a profound impact on how the reader understands and evaluates his character in the two versions. The Islamic Joseph is a man of faith whose master is Allah and who considers a tryst with the woman to constitute a breach of that relationship. The biblical Joseph has his sights set on more mundane matters. He, too, is aware of the theological repercussions should he give in, but he is first and foremost the servant of his human master and he frames the question with that relationship in mind. At this point the Bible reader is still not sure if Joseph even knows that the Lord, his other master, is with him.

Potiphar's character is totally unlike that of his counterpart in the Qur'an. He is present for all but the first two verses in the Islamic text and he plays a vital role in the plot. Each of the other characters speaks to him, and he pronounces the judgment that results in Joseph being exonerated and the woman chastised. As the story unfolds it is as if the reader is experiencing the action from the husband's perspective as he first discovers his wife with Joseph, then weighs the information he receives from the two of them and the witness, and finally renders a verdict. Throughout the narrative the focus of attention is on the husband and what his reaction will be.

In Genesis, Potiphar plays a different role in the narrative. He is mentioned by both Joseph (39:8-9) and his wife (39:14), but he does not actually appear until the last few verses after all the action has taken place. No one but his wife speaks to him in Genesis and, in a striking departure from his character in the Qur'an, he never utters a single word in this scene or anywhere else in the Bible. This is primarily due to the fact that he does not return home until after the attempted seduction and he only hears his wife's version of the events. In the biblical text the reader's primary question is what the woman's reaction to the situation will be. As she sits at home, Joseph's garment nearby, she has a number of options. Will she hold her silence and let the episode die, or will she falsely accuse Joseph to her husband? Whereas the Potiphar of the Qur'an is presented as a round and fully developed character who must exercise his reason and make a decision, his biblical alter ego is flatter and more passive: he is the one to whom his wife's decision is communicated.

Although he does not speak, Genesis describes Potiphar's response to his wife's report through the narrator, who says he became enraged (39:19). She plays the role of an innocent victim in convincing fashion and her husband falls for it hook, line, and sinker. But his anger is a curious reaction in light of what the reader already knows about Potiphar and his relationship with Joseph. This is the same man who, according to the always reliable narrator, saw that the Lord was with Joseph and entrusted all that he had to him (39:2-6). Why does he now rush to judgment and not even give Joseph the opportunity to defend himself? This is a gap in the narrative that leaves the reader wondering, and it becomes particularly apparent when we compare the two versions and note that the Islamic Potiphar exhibits an ability to judge the situation and evaluate it theologically that he lacks in Genesis.

Although they are relatively minor characters, the members of the household in the Bible also deserve mention. Like Potiphar, they are not physically present to witness what transpires between Joseph and the woman. Also like him, they get the wife's version of the events, thereby implicating Joseph and absolving her. Her reason for doing this is transparently obvious. When Joseph flees her presence she immediately summons them so that they will hear of it from her before Joseph can tell them what really happened. In this way the household members will be able to validate her story in the event that Potiphar should begin to ask them questions and inquire as to what they know.

She is not able to coach the household in the Qur'an. There one of them steps forward and proposes a way to get at the truth: if the shirt is torn from the back, the woman is guilty. The very group that is her ace up the sleeve in Genesis turns out to be the cause of her downfall in the Qur'an. This difference in how they are presented serves to put the woman in an even more negative light for the Bible reader. By getting to them before either Joseph or her husband can, she has succeeded in manipulating every other character in the narrative so that Joseph's guilt is a foregone conclusion.

The Guest of Honor (Qur'an 12:30-34)

The Qur'an's account of the attempted seduction has a brief sequel that recounts an unusual dinner party thrown by the wife.

> [30]The women in the city said, "The master's wife is trying to entice her young man. He has made her passionate. We think she is clearly in the wrong." [31]When she heard their comments, she sent to them and prepared a feast for them. She gave each one a knife and then said (to Joseph), "Come out to them!" When they saw him they exalted him and cut their hands saying, "Allah preserve us! This is no man—this is a noble angel!" [32]She said, "This is the one you blamed me for. I did try to entice him but he restrained himself. If he does not do what I order him to do he will be imprisoned and made worthless." [33]He said, "Oh Lord, I prefer prison to what they are asking me to do. Unless You turn back their plots from me, I will give in to them and become an unbeliever." [34]His Lord answered him and turned back their plots. Truly, He is the one who hears, the one who knows.

There is no parallel to this episode in Genesis, so it has no relevance for a comparative study of the Bible and the Qur'an. Nonetheless, there are a few things about this section of the Islamic text that warrant attention and consideration. First of all, while the story is not found in the Bible it is present in later Jewish literature. A number of different versions of the women's meal are found in rabbinic sources, and those texts share common elements with the Qurʾan's description of the gathering. For some scholars this phenomenon raises questions about sources and the possible influence of Jewish traditions on the Qurʾan. This is an interesting and important issue, but it lies outside the scope of our study. Because we are employing the method and tools of narrative criticism we are concerned only with the text as we have it and not its prehistory or possible sources.

This brief addendum to the Qurʾan seduction scene makes the wife both more sympathetic and more problematic for the reader. On the one hand, after being castigated as a sinner by her husband in the previous verse she is now further embarrassed by her friends, who mock her for having a crush on Joseph. She has become the laughingstock of her neighbors before she has had a chance to follow her husband's advice and admit her wrongdoing. This causes the reader to emotionally identify with her as a tragic figure who deserves some level of sympathy.

In the same way, the fact that all of these women are immediately attracted to Joseph serves to explain, if not excuse, why the wife attempted to entice him. He has the capacity to make women swoon, and the reader is left with the sense that many women would be tempted to do the same thing she did if given the opportunity.

Still, there are things about the woman that make her hard to like. Her demand that Joseph obey her and give in to her wishes (v. 32) indicates that she still has not learned her lesson after being caught and publicly exposed. In addition, she remains clueless about why Joseph was able to withstand her advances, and attributes it to his powers of self-control (v. 32). The reader knows that, in fact, Joseph's determination has a divine source since he would have given in if Allah had not come to his aid (v. 24). Ironically, the woman continues to remain unaware of that truth even as the deity answers Joseph's prayer for help in overcoming the group of women who now seek to seduce him (v. 34).

The dinner scene continues the theme of plotting that we have already identified elsewhere in the Qurʾan's Joseph story. In v. 33 Joseph prays that Allah might turn back their plots, and this is precisely what happens in the next verse. The plural form "their plots" is found in both of these verses and recalls her husband's words to the woman in v. 28. In that earlier scene he used the second-person plural form "your plots" twice, and we noted that this is a curious mode of address since he is speaking only to his wife. In light of what takes place at the dinner party and the double reference to "their plots" there, it is best to see the husband's words as anticipating what will happen in the next scene when a group of women plot against Joseph.

The section ends by calling attention to Allah's ability to be aware of all that occurs: "Truly He is the one who hears, the one who knows." The reference to Allah's knowledge continues a major motif of the Islamic story of Joseph. Just as the section treated in the previous chapter ended with a reference to the deity knowing what they did to Joseph (v. 19), this one concludes with another allusion to divine knowledge. In between, Allah grants Joseph wisdom and knowledge (v. 22), and intervenes in Joseph's affairs in a way that indicates the deity's awareness of what is happening to him.

The consistent presence of this theme in the Islamic text makes its relative absence in Genesis more obvious. God is mentioned for the first time in this part of the biblical Joseph story, but the divine character remains fairly flat and undeveloped. Apart from Joseph's comment about sinning against God in v. 9, the only other places where the deity is mentioned occur early in the chapter when it is said that God is with Joseph and is the reason for the success that both he and Potiphar experience. But what does God know? How exactly is God with Joseph? Does God intervene when Joseph is tempted? These are questions that are addressed in the Qur'an but left unanswered in Genesis.

CHAPTER THREE

Events: Joseph and the Prisoners
(Genesis 39:20–40:23; Qur'an 12:35-42)

The next place Joseph finds himself is in prison, where he encounters two fellow inmates who have unusual dreams. This part of the Joseph story in the Bible can be divided into two sections. The first describes Joseph's arrival in prison and his relationship with the two men, and the second treats the dreams and their interpretation. The Qur'an account of the episode follows a similar if somewhat abbreviated structure.

In our analysis of this material we will pay special attention to how the various events of each story interrelate. Events serve as the building blocks of a narrative because they describe the action and give structure to the plot. One of the most important issues to consider when engaging in narrative criticism is how each event relates to previous and subsequent ones. In particular, the question of causality is critical. Is a certain event the result of some other event that happened earlier in the narrative? Is it the cause of another event that takes place later in the narrative? Or does there not appear to be any causal relationship between one particular event and others? Plots are story lines that trace such connections; events are often contingent upon previous ones and, in turn, help to bring about future events.

A number of examples of this can be seen in the portion of the Genesis Joseph story that has already been studied. The hatred Joseph's brothers feel toward him is the result of his being Jacob's favorite son. That hatred becomes the cause of his being left in the well, which then becomes the cause of his being rescued and brought to Potiphar's house. The Lord being with Joseph is what enables Potiphar to entrust Joseph with his possessions. This trust is what allows Joseph to be alone with the woman, thus leading to the attempted seduction. And, of course, the failed seduction is what lands Joseph in prison.

Readers usually expect a narrative to follow certain conventions as the events of a plot are described. In other words, there are particular rules and formats that are typically used in the telling of a story. For example, it is common for a narrative to unfold in a more or less chronological order in which prior events are related before subsequent ones. Similarly, the relationships among those events are often fairly clear so that the reader has a sense of where causality and contingency are present in the plot. These and similar conventions that are predictable and expected usually contribute to the reader's ability to follow the action and make sense of a narrative.

At times the conventions are ignored or played with in order to achieve a particular effect. For instance, flashback is a common device that breaks the temporal sequence by introducing material that is chronologically prior to what is being reported. Sometimes the events are related in an order that bears little resemblance to their actual occurrence, and this can have an unsettling, even confusing effect on the reader. Two examples of this technique can be seen in the films *Pulp Fiction* and *Memento,* which violate the normal conventions in ways that make it difficult for the viewer to understand how the events of the narrative relate to one another. Despite the difficulties inherent in this type of chronological arrangement, such a presentation can also have certain benefits. Most viewers of these films have spoken in positive terms of their unusual ordering of events and the powerful impression this technique leaves.

Prison Chains (of Events)
(Genesis 39:20–40:8; Qurʾan 12:35-36a)

Biblical narrative never reorders the sequence in the radical way these films do, but an analysis of how it presents the relationships among events can often yield interesting results. When we consider how Joseph's experience in prison is recounted in the two books it is clear that the Genesis version pays more attention to causality than the Qurʾan does. There is a strong sense of interconnection among the various events of the biblical narrative that makes each one contingent upon what comes before it. This can be seen in the first section, describing Joseph's arrival in prison and his relationship with the other two prisoners, which is found in Gen 39:20–40:8:

> [20]And Joseph's master took him and put him into the prison, the place where the king's prisoners were confined; he remained there in prison. [21]But the Lord was with Joseph and showed him steadfast love; he gave him favor in the sight of the chief jailer. [22]The chief jailer committed to Joseph's care all the prisoners who were in the prison, and whatever was done there, he was the one who did it. [23]The chief jailer paid no heed to anything that was in Joseph's care, because the Lord was with

him; and whatever he did, the Lord made him prosper. ⁴⁰:¹Some time after this, the cupbearer of the king of Egypt and his baker offended their lord the king of Egypt. ²Pharaoh was angry with his two officers, the chief cupbearer and the chief baker, ³and he put them in custody in the house of the captain of the guard, in the prison where Joseph was confined. ⁴The captain of the guard charged Joseph with them, and he waited on them; and they continued for some time in custody. ⁵One night they both dreamed—the cupbearer and the baker of the king of Egypt, who were confined in the prison—each his own dream, and each dream with its own meaning. ⁶When Joseph came to them in the morning, he saw that they were troubled. ⁷So he asked Pharaoh's officers, who were with him in custody in his master's house, "Why are your faces downcast today?" ⁸They said to him, "We have had dreams, and there is no one to interpret them." And Joseph said to them, "Do not interpretations belong to God? Please tell them to me."

This section describes a chain of events that are mostly linked by causality and contingency. In other words, things happen because something else has happened previously. The following chart identifies some of the clearest examples of this cause-and-effect pattern.

EVENT	RESULT
Joseph is imprisoned	The Lord is with him
The Lord is with Joseph	Chief jailer puts all in Joseph's charge
The two men offend Pharaoh	Pharaoh imprisons them
Joseph is charged with the two men	He waits on them
The two men dream	They are troubled
The two men are troubled	Joseph asks them what is wrong

The overall structure of the section is organized around the principle of causality whereby most events build upon or are shaped by the ones prior to it. An examination of vv. 20 through 23 shows that this feature extends beneath the major events of the narrative and is also present on a microlevel. Note the sequence of events in the following list and how each one is contingent upon what comes before it.

1. Joseph is imprisoned.
2. The Lord is with Joseph.

3. The Lord shows Joseph steadfast love.
4. The Lord gives Joseph favor in the sight of the chief jailer.
5. The chief jailer commits all the prisoners to Joseph's care.
6. The chief jailer pays no attention to what is in Joseph's care.

The principle of causality is also operative in the relationship between this section and the previous one because Joseph's imprisonment is contingent upon what happens after the attempted seduction. Potiphar's anger against Joseph and his decision to have him thrown into jail are the result of what his wife reports to him about what transpired between her and Joseph. It is quite clear, then, that the events of this portion of the Genesis Joseph story are presented in a logical and ordered way that allows the reader to see the causal relationships among them.

As we consider this section in relation to the previous one we also detect a pattern in the way Joseph's story is told in the Bible. A similar series of events is narrated both in Potiphar's house and in the prison to explain how Joseph is able to rise in status despite his difficult state of affairs. In each case, as soon as Joseph arrives in his new environment it is said that the Lord is with him (39:2, 21). This leads to his finding favor in the eyes of his superior with the result that he is put in a position of authority (39:4, 22). The ultimate outcome of his new status is success for both Joseph and his surroundings (39:5, 23). We will find that this pattern continues in the next section when Joseph is released from prison and enters Pharaoh's household.

The repetition of this sequence gives a certain coherence and structure to the biblical narrative that has an impact on the reader. In the first place, it contributes to the image of Joseph as a figure with the ability to thrive in any situation and rise above the most trying circumstances. Nothing—not the bottom of a well, Potiphar's house, or prison—can hold him down or prevent others from recognizing his special qualities. In addition, there is the theological aspect of each of these scenes. Joseph's prosperity is intimately tied to the presence of God in his life, and the repetition of this motif in successive scenes encourages the reader to think of Joseph as a person who enjoys a privileged relationship with God. At the same time it enhances the character of the deity as a God whose influence is not limited to the land of Israel but extends into the foreign territory of Egypt.

Describing Joseph's success in prison in a way that echoes his rise in Potiphar's house also raises a red flag in the reader's mind. Will the outcome of the two scenes be the same? Since they both start the same way, the reader cannot help but ask if they will end the same way with Joseph being the victim of someone else's manipulation as he was in Potiphar's house. This is one of the results of the use of patterns in narratives. The reader is already familiar with the outcome of a similar set of events that was related earlier and wonders if the pattern will hold or be broken the next time around. This is a standard device in stories like fairy tales ("Goldilocks and the Three Bears," for example) that make use of patterns and repetition to great effect. As we will see, there is good reason for the reader to conclude that Joseph will be a victim in prison as he was in Potiphar's house, until an unexpected turn of events moves the narrative in a different direction.

There is no doubt at all in the Bible reader's mind about how and why Joseph ends up in prison because this information comes from the narrator who is always reliable and trustworthy. This is similar to what we saw in 39:1-6, where the narrator's voice provides all the background material necessary to understand the events in Potiphar's house. But there is some question about the time component of the prison scene. For example, the narrated time is unexpressed in 39:20-23 and we have no idea how much time passes between the beginning and the end of that section. The author calls attention to this fact by beginning the next verse with the words "Some time after this. . . ." There is a similar lack of specificity in other phrases like "some time" (v. 4) and "one night" (v. 5) that make it impossible to know exactly how much time Joseph spends in jail in Genesis. This underscores an interesting aspect of how Genesis presents the narrative in this part of the Joseph story. It goes to great lengths to establish the sequential and causal relationships among the different events described, but it does not identify the period of time in which they occur.

The reference to the dreams of the prisoners establishes a link with the beginning of the Genesis story when Joseph himself has two dreams (37:5-11), and the same motif will reappear in the next section with Pharaoh's two dreams. These three sets of double dreams serve to unify the narrative and show how the repetition of similar events throughout a story can focus the reader's attention on key themes. In the present case those themes appear to be the nature of dreams as communications from God, and the importance of interpreting dreams in order to unlock the messages they contain.

Joseph states in v. 8 that interpretations belong to God, but this did not appear to be the case in ch. 37 after he had his two dreams. In that chapter it is human beings, not the deity, who explain the meanings of the dreams. The brothers interpret Joseph's first dream about the sheaves as an expression of his superiority over them (37:8). Similarly, Jacob explicates the second dream involving the sun, moon, and stars in a way that places Joseph over the rest of the family (37:10). Perhaps his comment that interpretations belong to God is the text's way of critiquing these attempts by his family members to explain the dreams and therefore remind the reader that this is a power reserved only for the deity.

When Joseph says that interpretations belong to God and then asks the two men to tell him their dreams, what is he saying about himself? The statement appears to be a claim that he has access to knowledge that is unique to God. Does he believe God has given him the power of interpretation? Up to this point in the Genesis narrative Joseph has been a dreamer, not an interpreter. His brothers say as much before throwing him into the pit: "Here comes this dreamer" (37:19). We have already noted that even though it is stated repeatedly in both Potiphar's house (39:2-6) and in prison (39:21-23) that the Lord is with Joseph, the narrator does not say that Joseph himself knows this. Consequently, when he asks his fellow prisoners to tell him their dreams he is revealing a level of knowledge and awareness about himself that was previously unknown to the reader.

To put it another way, Joseph's request to hear the dreams lacks the element of causality that is a characteristic feature of this section of the Genesis story. Up to this point each event is contingent upon what has come before it, and the causal connections have been clearly identified for the reader. Here, when Joseph says interpretations are from God and then asks the men to tell him their dreams, the cause-and-effect relationship is not immediately apparent. The reader must infer from Joseph's words not only that he knows God is with him, but that he has been given special knowledge from the deity. The Bible reader has to read between the lines and connect the dots in a way the Qur'an reader does not, because the Islamic text plainly states that Allah gave Joseph wisdom and knowledge and taught him the interpretation of events (vv. 21-22).

The Qur'an's version of these events in vv. 35-36a is quite brief and lacks the narrative detail found in Genesis. "Then, even after seeing the signs, they thought it well to imprison him for a time. Two young men were imprisoned with him." The Islamic text provides no information on the chief jailer, the two men, or how they end up in prison. Likewise, the element of causality that is such a central component of the biblical story is not found here. The narrator recounts just two events—Joseph is put in prison and two other men are imprisoned with him—and there is no cause-and-effect relationship between them. Of course, the same thing can be said about the biblical account where the imprisonment of the cupbearer and baker (40:1) is not contingent upon an earlier event. But we have noted that the bulk of the Genesis material is organized around a chain of events with each one dependent upon or caused by what comes before it. There is no such causality in the Qur'an passage.

In fact, v. 35 appears to underscore this lack of causality by calling attention to the random nature of the events described. Imprisoning Joseph is not the logical action one should take after seeing the signs, but he is sent to jail anyway. When we consider this in light of the previous narrative in the Qur'an the absence of causality becomes more obvious and mystifying. At first glance there does not appear to be any reason why the Islamic Joseph should end up in prison. Unlike his biblical counterpart, he is exonerated by his master and not found guilty of the charges against him. The master's wife even comes clean and admits her responsibility and guilt to the other women (v. 32). Given that sequence of events, why is Joseph punished instead of the wife?

A possible answer to this question might be found in v. 33 when Joseph prays, "Oh Lord, I prefer prison to what they are asking me to do. Unless You turn back their plots from me, I will give in to them and become an unbeliever." The next verse goes on to say that Allah answered Joseph and turned back the women's plots. Perhaps Joseph goes to prison because this is precisely what he prayed for. The woman states that if Joseph does not comply with her wishes she will have him incarcerated (v. 32), and he favors this alternative to giving in and rejecting his faith.

This interpretation of the events introduces a theological dimension to the imprisonment that is present in the Bible but otherwise absent from the Qur'an. It has already been observed that the Genesis account stresses the idea that God is with Joseph and is the reason behind his success while he is in jail (39:21-23). The Islamic text does not make this same claim, but seeing Joseph's imprisonment as a response to his prayer enables the reader to infer a level of divine involvement in the text even if it is not stated as explicitly as it is in Genesis. This reading will be affirmed when we examine the next scene, where it is clear that Allah is with Joseph in prison.

We have noted that the reference to the men's dreams in the Genesis passage reminds the reader of the beginning of the story when Joseph himself has two dreams. So, too, in the Qur'an text the reader's attention is directed back to an earlier point in the narrative. The mention of "signs" in v. 35 is somewhat enigmatic, as is the identification of those who saw them as "they." What exactly were these signs and who saw them? Joseph does not do anything that is identified as a sign either during the attempted seduction or in the later scene with the women at the dinner party.

The attentive reader will recall that this is not the first time the word "signs" is used in the Qur'an's Joseph story. In v. 7 it was said: "In Joseph and his brothers there are signs for those who inquire." That verse is directed to the reader, who is instructed to inquire about the deeper meaning of the story of Joseph and his brothers in order to learn its true significance. This second use of the term "signs" continues the same theme. It says that when "they" (certainly the wife, possibly her husband, maybe others) imprison Joseph they are guilty of misreading the signs and not properly inquiring of them. Had they correctly understood what Joseph was saying and doing, they never would have reached the decision to have him imprisoned. In this way "they" personify those who are unable to inquire of the story and arrive at an understanding of its deeper meaning.

This comparative analysis of the first part of the prison scene has shown that Genesis presents a more detailed narrative that pays close attention to the relationships among the events it describes, thereby facilitating the reader's understanding of the story. The Qurʾan's account, while not incoherent, leaves some questions in the reader's mind because it is lacking in detail and does not articulate as precisely how the events of the narrative relate to each other.

This is most easily seen in the discrepancy between the numbers of events reported in each version: what is conveyed through two events in the Islamic text is spread out over twenty in Genesis. The basic outline is the same in both, since each describes the imprisonment of Joseph and the two men. But there is a world of difference in the details, because the reader of the Qurʾan is not given any further information. The Bible reader, on the other hand, learns a great deal more from ten times as many events that describe how God, Joseph, and the men interact.

Good News and Bad News (Genesis 40:9-23; Qurʾan 12:36b-42)

The second part of the Qurʾan's description of Joseph's stay in prison, which describes the dreams and their interpretation, is found in vv. 36b-42. Here, too, the causal connections among the various events are sometimes not immediately apparent, and this results in a narrative that does not flow smoothly in places.

> ³⁶One of them said, "I saw myself in a dream pressing grapes." The other said, "I dreamt I was carrying bread upon my head and birds were eating from it. Tell us the meaning of this. We see you are a good man." ³⁷He said, "The food that is given to you will not arrive before I tell you the meaning. This is one of the things my Lord has taught me. I have left the religion of those who do not believe in Allah and those who deny the world to come. ³⁸I follow the religion of my fathers Abraham, Isaac, and Jacob. We do not associate anything with Allah. This is one of Allah's favors to us and to all people, but most people are not thankful. ³⁹Oh my fellow prisoners, are many gods better than Allah the one, the all-powerful? ⁴⁰What you worship apart from Him are nothing but names that you and your fathers have given. Allah has revealed no authority for them. Judgment belongs only to Allah. He commands that you worship none but Him. That is the proper faith, but most people

do not know. ⁴¹Oh my fellow prisoners, one of you will serve his master wine, while the other will be crucified and birds will peck at his head. The matter you have asked about has been decided." ⁴²He said to the one he knew would be released, "Remember me to your master." But Satan caused him to forget to mention it to his master and Joseph remained in prison for some years.

There is a rather abrupt transition to the dreams in this Qur'an passage. The text introduces the two men in the beginning of v. 36 and then has them immediately relate the content of their dreams to Joseph. The Genesis account, on the other hand, presents a series of events that lead up to this moment. The Bible reader is told that the men each have a dream on the same night, Joseph sees they are troubled and asks them why, and they tell him they have had dreams that they do not understand. Only at this point does Joseph ask them to tell him their dreams.

The Islamic text has them relate their dreams to Joseph one after another without explaining why they do so. Unlike in Genesis, Joseph does not see that his fellow prisoners are troubled, and he does not ask them to tell him their dreams. They, not Joseph, take the initiative: "Tell us the meaning of this." The reason they say this is because they see he is "a good man" (v. 36). But how do they know this? The text does not provide any information regarding how long and in what capacity they have known Joseph, so the reader is left in the dark as to how they have determined he is a good man. The Qur'an's lack of causal connections that would help explain why things happen leads to an unevenness in the narrative that disrupts its flow in places.

The two men and Joseph refer to his ability to determine the meaning of the dreams (vv. 36, 37). The Arabic word translated as "meaning" *(ta'wīl)* is also found in vv. 6 and 21 where Jacob and the divine narrator refer to Joseph's capacity to interpret events. In both those earlier verses it is stated that Allah is the one who gives Joseph this power, and Joseph acknowledges the source of this ability when he says in v. 37, "This is one of the things my Lord has taught me." This is the Qur'an's equivalent of Joseph's statement in Genesis that all interpretations belong to God (40:8), and it may be his way of informing his fellow prisoners that, even though he is a good man, he would be unable to interpret their dreams without Allah's help.

Joseph then launches into a mini-sermon (vv. 37b-40) that appears to come out of the blue. The two men have asked for his help in understanding their dreams, but Joseph proceeds to lecture them on the nature of true faith. On the surface level this seems to be unconnected to what has come before it, but it may be a continuation of Joseph's comment that the interpretation of dreams is one of the things his Lord has taught him. Before granting their request Joseph wishes to tell them about the other things his Lord has taught him, the most important being proper belief.

This is in keeping with Joseph's role as a prophet in Islam. According to the Muslim understanding of revelation, throughout history Allah has chosen individuals to communicate the divine message and call people to proper faith. Joseph is among those chosen ones, and his words to his fellow prisoners are in line with what the Qur'an reports other prophets have said to their own people. He urges his listeners to reject polytheism and embrace worship of the one true God who is the supreme judge and ruler of all. By placing himself in line with Abraham, Isaac, and Jacob he affirms the close ties that exist between Islam and the religions of the Bible, a theme that is frequently addressed in Islam's sacred text. The sermon ends on a familiar note: "That is the proper faith, but most people do not know." We have seen that knowledge or its absence is a recurring theme throughout the Joseph story in the Qur'an, and here the main character mentions its importance in matters of faith.

The prominence of Joseph's theological discourse can be seen in the fact that it comprises a little more than one-half of the entire words in this section. In fact, it is the longest speech Joseph gives in the entire story in the Qur'an. This is in marked contrast to Genesis, where Joseph mentions God on occasion but never delivers an extended theological address as he does in the Qur'an. The significance of this difference, and the impact it has on how the reader perceives Joseph's character, will be discussed in our analysis of the Genesis version of the events. For now it should be noted that Joseph's speech conveys the idea that God is with him, something that is communicated through the narrator in the Bible rather than by the character himself.

After his excursus on religious faith is concluded, Joseph turns to the dreams and their meaning (v. 41). His interpretation is brief and to the point, lacking the dramatic element we will note in the biblical parallel. Its sparseness is striking in light of the detail with which he has just described the nature of true faith and the passion with which he has urged the men to embrace it. This difference also suggests that the lesson in faith, rather than what Joseph has to say about the dreams, is the main thing the reader should take away from the text.

Joseph's interpretation of the dreams subtly serves his theological agenda. He follows his explanation of their meaning with the comment, "The matter you have asked about has been decided." The Arabic expression "the matter has been decided" *(quḍiya al-amr)* is an example of the "divine passive," and the phrase appears with some regularity in the Qur'an. It usually conveys the idea that Allah has already determined the outcome of a particular event and the situation is now out of human hands. Its use here expresses the complete authority of Allah and indicates that the interpretation Joseph has just put forward will come to pass. In a passage that tends to be silent about the reasons why certain events come to pass, here we have a statement of divine causality that is unambiguous and certain.

But Allah is not the only non-human agent of causality who is identified in this passage. The section ends with a reference to Satan as the reason why the released prisoner neglects to tell his master about Joseph. The reader is immediately reminded of Jacob's words to Joseph back in v. 5, when he warns him, "Truly, Satan is a clear enemy to people." The truth of Jacob's statement is now apparent as Joseph is forced to spend additional years in prison because of what Satan has done.

The longer and more detailed biblical version of the dreams and their interpretations is found in Gen 40:9-23:

> [9]So the chief cupbearer told his dream to Joseph, and said to him, "In my dream there was a vine before me, [10]and on the vine there were three branches. As soon as it budded, its blossoms came out and the clusters ripened into grapes. [11]Pharaoh's cup was in my hand; and I took the grapes and pressed them into Pharaoh's cup, and placed the cup in Pharaoh's hand." [12]Then Joseph said to him, "This is its interpretation: the three branches are three days; [13]within three days Pharaoh will lift up your head and restore you to your office; and you shall place Pharaoh's cup in his hand, just as you used to do when you were his cupbearer. [14]But remember me when it is well with you; please do me the kindness to make mention of me to Pharaoh, and so get me out of this place. [15]For in fact I was stolen out of the land of the Hebrews; and here also I have done nothing that they should have put me into the dungeon."
>
> [16]When the chief baker saw that the interpretation was favorable, he said to Joseph, "I also had a dream: there were three cake baskets on my head, [17]and in the uppermost basket there were all sorts of baked food for Pharaoh, but the birds were eating it out of the basket on my head." [18]And Joseph answered, "This is its interpretation: the three baskets are three days; [19]within three days Pharaoh will lift up your head—from you!— and hang you on a pole; and the birds will eat the flesh from you."
>
> [20]On the third day, which was Pharaoh's birthday, he made a feast for all his servants, and lifted up the head of the chief cupbearer and the head of the chief baker among his servants. [21]He restored the chief cupbearer to his cupbearing, and he placed the cup in Pharaoh's hand; [22]but the chief baker he hanged, just as Joseph had interpreted to them. [23]Yet the chief cupbearer did not remember Joseph, but forgot him.

The flow of events in Genesis is more even than it is in the Qur'an, and the causality between them is clearer. For example, the men tell Joseph about their dreams because he has asked them to do so, while in the Islamic text they relate their dreams to him without being prompted. There is a pattern to the order of the biblical events that suggests a cause-and-effect relationship among them. The cupbearer relates his dream and Joseph immediately offers his interpretation of it. This is followed by a description of the baker's dream and its interpretation. The narrator clearly states that the baker's decision to tell Joseph his dream is contingent upon Joseph's explanation of the first dream: "When the chief baker saw that the interpretation was favorable, he said to Joseph. . . ."

The Qur'an account lacks this sense of one event building upon another because of the way it is organized. Rather than the order dream #1, interpretation #1, dream #2, interpretation #2, the Islamic text reports the two dreams together and then the two interpretations together. These two units are divided by Joseph's rather lengthy theological speech that occurs between the description of the dreams and their interpretation, a placement that disrupts the narrative flow of the story. The plot of the Genesis story, on the other hand, is clearly built on the principle that each episode is the result of what comes before it:

Joseph's request to hear the dreams (40:8)
The cupbearer's dream (40:9-11)
Joseph's interpretation of the cupbearer's dream (40:12-15)
The baker's dream (40:16-17)
Joseph's interpretation of the baker's dream (40:18-19)

The pattern continues with the description of Pharaoh's birthday feast (40:20-23), not found in the Qur'an, that comes right after the second dream and explains how it is that Joseph's interpretations will come to pass. The party might even be seen as an occasion of causality since it provides the opportunity for the Egyptian ruler to call together all of his servants for a gathering that seals the fates of the cupbearer and the baker. It is clear, then, that the biblical narrative is constructed in a way that stresses its interconnections. In Genesis, Joseph's stay in prison is presented in the form of an interlocking chain of events that follow each other in logical and orderly succession.

It has already been noted that causality is particularly evident in the description of the baker's dream and its interpretation. This is a brief but poignant scene in which the character is a victim of his mistaken understanding of the cause-and-effect nature of the events. The narrator begins by offering the reader a glimpse into the mind of the baker. "When the chief baker saw that the interpretation was favorable. . . ." This comment leaves the impression that the baker would have been reluctant to divulge the contents of his dream if the interpretation of the first one had not been positive. In other words, the baker assumes that his dream and the cupbearer's will be interpreted along similar lines.

The reason for that assumption is the similarity of the two dreams. While not identical, they share certain features in common. The number three, Pharaoh, and sources of sustenance (grapes, baked goods) are all elements of both dreams. In addition, each man's dream is related to the function he serves in Pharaoh's household. These are the very aspects of the cupbearer's dream that Joseph mentions in his interpretation, so the baker believes that his dream will also receive a favorable explanation. He is, of course, wrong in that assumption, and the way he and the reader discover that error is a fine example of the narrative artistry contained in the Bible.

With the narrator's help, the reader comes to know the baker in the most intimate of ways: by entering his head and discovering his thoughts. This creates a bond between the reader and the character. In effect, the reader experiences the events of the story from the baker's perspective and comes to identify with him through that shared point of view. A similar bond develops between the cupbearer and the reader, but it is relatively shallow in nature. The cupbearer reports the contents of his dream and this enables the reader to see the dream from his perspective, but that experience lacks the immediacy and closeness the reader feels when the baker sees that the first interpretation is positive and then decides to describe his own dream. The reader is not privy to the reactions and feelings of the cupbearer in this same way, and so he remains a more distant character. The presence of just a few words from the narrator at the beginning of v. 16 completely transforms how the reader relates to the baker.

There is a tragic quality to the baker's character that causes the reader to feel sympathy for him. The man gets his hopes up only to have them dashed, and we cannot help but feel sorry for him. The fact that his co-worker in Pharaoh's court will be released only adds to the tragedy and increases the reader's sense of pity.

Perhaps the most effective device employed to enhance the reader's sympathy for the baker is the author's use of repetition. After he describes his dream, the baker hears words from Joseph that appear to confirm his hunch that he will be set free. Joseph begins his interpretation of the baker's dream with the very same words that he spoke when he interpreted the cupbearer's dream. The first nineteen words (fourteen in the Hebrew text) of the interpretations are identical except for the substitution of the word "baskets" (v. 18) for "branches" (v. 12). The similar nature of the two dreams and Joseph's use of the same words to begin his interpretation of both lead the baker (and the reader) to assume that he, too, will be restored to his office. Up to the words "Pharaoh will lift up your head" the baker expects to be back in his master's good graces. But the words that follow—"from you!"—suddenly pull the rug out from under him and tell him that his fate will be very different from that of his fellow servant.

The reader, who already identifies with the baker, is also caught off guard by this unexpected turn of events. This is partly a function of the strong presence of causality in the narrative up to this point. There has been an orderly progression throughout the course of the story as each event is contingent upon what has come before it. The reader expects this same principle to be operative for the interpretation of the baker's dream. Because the dream contains some of the same elements as the cupbearer's and Joseph's interpretation of each begins in exactly the same way, the reader assumes the outcome will be the same in both cases. When it is not, the reader, like the character, is taken by surprise and is left with the feeling of having been set up by Joseph and the narrator to anticipate the opposite result.

One reason why this works so effectively is that there is a gap in the biblical narrative that prevents the reader from having full information. The only things that are different about these two men are their occupations and their dreams. The text does not differentiate them in any other way. This comes out clearly in the circumstances that lead up to their incarceration: they both offend their master, and Pharaoh becomes angry with both of them (40:1-2). The reader does not know what exactly they did to offend the Egyptian ruler and whether or not they are both guilty of the same offense. Because no distinction is made between them on these matters, the tendency is to assume they acted in tandem to upset their master. The reader therefore expects the outcomes of both their cases to be the same. When the cupbearer's dream is interpreted favorably, the logical assumption is that the explanation of the baker's dream will follow suit, but it does not.

If the reader had additional knowledge about the two men, their different fates might come as less of a surprise. Background information on the nature of their offense or the relationship each one had with Pharaoh would help to contextualize their situations and put the reader in a better position to evaluate them as characters and to anticipate how the story might end. But the narrator chooses to divulge only a limited amount of information about them, thereby introducing a level of ambiguity that has a significant bearing on how the reader understands the events and relates to the characters. It is interesting to note that this gap in knowledge is never filled and continues until the end of the Genesis story. Even at Pharaoh's birthday party the reader is not told why he chooses to release the cupbearer and have the baker killed.

When we compare the biblical version of events with the way the Qur'an describes them, the lack of a theological component is one of the most obvious differences. The mini-sermon Joseph delivers to his fellow prisoners is the focal point of the Islamic text, and it has no counterpart in Genesis. But that does not mean the biblical Joseph does not display his oratorical skills in order to persuade his audience. He does so, but with a completely different agenda. Rather than talk about God, Joseph talks about himself.

The Islamic Joseph asks the prisoner who will be released, "Remember me to your master," a brief request that is communicated in only three words in the original Arabic text. But the biblical Joseph extends this considerably in vv. 14 and 15 by not only making the same petition but also explaining why it should be granted. Joseph appeals to the cupbearer's sense of justice and attempts to persuade him by pointing out that he, Joseph, does not deserve to be in prison. He then takes it a step further and informs the cupbearer that he should not even be in Egypt, let alone this jail. "For in fact I was stolen out of the land of the Hebrews; and here also I have done nothing that they should have put me into the dungeon." The connection between his present predicament and the mistreatment he received at the hands of his brothers is strengthened in Genesis through the use of repetition. The Hebrew word translated as "dungeon" *(bōr)* is the same one that was used in ch. 37 to describe the pit into which Joseph was thrown. He understands his current imprisonment to be the equivalent of the time he spent in the empty well he occupied earlier, and he sees himself as a victim in both cases.

This is the first time the reader is told what Joseph thinks about his situation. The descriptions of his being sold into Egypt and cast into prison do not make a single reference to his reactions or thoughts. Only here, long after the events themselves, does the reader learn of Joseph's sense of betrayal and mistreatment. Up to this point in the biblical narrative the main character's thoughts and feelings have remained something of a mystery. The one place that offers a glimpse of what is going on in his mind is in the scene with Potiphar's wife when he explains his reason for rejecting her advances (39:8-9). But his words there are in the form of a rather objective and theoretical argument that demonstrates Joseph's analytical ability without revealing his emotions. The Bible reader is finally exposed to Joseph's feelings here, in the conversation with the cupbearer.

The way this is done, and the impact it has on the reader, is similar to what has already been noted with regard to the baker. The information is presented from Joseph's perspective in his own words, and this causes the reader to adopt his point of view and identify with the character. Joseph's comment in v. 15: "for in fact I was stolen out of the land of the Hebrews; and here also I have done nothing that they should have put me into the dungeon" is a complaint heavy with emotion that reveals much about his character. It is also a statement that agrees with the reader's view of things, because Joseph has been presented as an innocent victim throughout the Genesis account. This shared assessment, now verbally articulated by Joseph, helps to strengthen the bond between reader and character.

Point of view is a very important component of narrative study that will be discussed in more detail in a later chapter. It is important to note here how quickly the reader's perspective can change as the narrator shifts from one point of view to another. The transition between vv. 15 and 16 in the present text is an excellent example of this. We have seen that v. 15 expresses Joseph's thoughts and emotions in a way that causes the reader to see things from his perspective and identify with him. But the reader is not allowed to stay in that position for long. In the very next verse the baker's point of view is adopted, and the reader begins to see the events of the narrative from his perspective.

Interestingly, the element of causality between events that, up to this point, has been a hallmark of this section of the biblical story is no longer operative. This is seen when Joseph calls attention to the lack of any cause for his present situation. He has done nothing to deserve being imprisoned in Egypt and is at a loss to explain how such a thing could have happened to him. In effect his claim of innocence in Genesis is an attempt to tell his fellow prisoners that he is a "good man," an assessment they volunteer in the Qur'an without any prompting from him (v. 36).

This difference raises an important question for the Bible reader—what do the men know about Joseph? In the Islamic text they know he is a good man, and the mini-sermon he delivers tells them he is a man of faith. All they know in Genesis, if they believe him, is that he has been unfairly imprisoned. The absence of any explicitly theological material makes it impossible for them to formulate an opinion about his spiritual life. Even the references to God being with him and his comment that interpretations belong to God (40:8) lack the detail necessary to reach a conclusion about his faith life.

Causality is also lacking in the last event narrated in the biblical text. According to the Qur'an, Satan is the reason why the released prisoner forgets about Joseph (v. 42), but Genesis offers no such explanation and simply says that the man forgot him. The cupbearer's oversight is particularly unusual in light of the fact that the biblical Joseph, unlike his Islamic counterpart, goes to some lengths to assert his innocence to the man, making it more likely that the cupbearer would remember him. This disruption of a pattern that runs through the biblical version raises another issue: why did the cupbearer forget? The Bible reader never discovers the answer.

CHAPTER FOUR

Repetition: Joseph and Pharaoh (Genesis 41:1-45; Qurʾan 12:43-57)

According to both the Bible and the Qurʾan, Joseph is eventually released from prison when the man whose dream he interpreted favorably remembers to mention him to Pharaoh. Upon being freed, Joseph is brought to the Egyptian ruler's court where he has an audience with the most powerful figure in the country. It is a dramatic high point in the narrative that has a significant bearing on the direction and shape of Joseph's future. It is also an important scene because the description of this initial encounter with Pharaoh contains a number of examples of repetition, one of the most common literary devices found in the Bible.

Repetition has been identified in a number of places in the parts of the Joseph story we have already studied. In the Qurʾan it was noted in the two references to Satan (vv. 5, 42), the frequent use of terminology associated with knowledge, and the several places where the theme of plotting is mentioned (vv. 5, 28, 33). Examples of repetition in Genesis have been seen in the reoccurrence of the motif of Joseph's clothing (37:3, 33; 39:12), the multiple dreams in the story (37:5-11; 40:9-19), and the pattern of Joseph rising to a position of authority and trust because the Lord is with him.

The present chapter will study this important device in greater detail, and it will attempt to explain the different ways repetition can function in a story by examining the role it plays in the scene between Joseph and Pharaoh. Modern readers sometimes find repetition to be an unappealing or annoying aspect of biblical narrative. It can strike them as an unnecessary and redundant rehearsal of familiar information, and on occasion Bible scholars have concurred with this assessment. Some consider the biblical penchant for repetition, especially verbatim retelling, to be a vestige from the past that indicates the archaic nature of the material. This allows them to reach certain untenable conclusions about the minds and cultures of ancient peoples. Other scholars take repetition to be evidence of different sources behind the text. In this view the writer is more like an editor or redactor who combines various types of material into a final product whose seams and junctures can be ascertained through the presence of repetition.

Such approaches fail to appreciate the true nature and purpose of repetition in the Bible and elsewhere. It is not best explained by appealing to the age of a text, the mind of its author, or the prior sources upon which it has allegedly drawn. One must look first at how it functions within the text and what kind of contribution it makes to the reader's ability to understand and interpret the story. As we will see, both the Qur'an and the Bible make very effective use of repetition in ways that facilitate the reading experience and allow them to achieve their separate purposes.

The brief listing found above illustrates the fact that there are different types of repetition. Sometimes individual words or phrases are repeated, and at other times particular motifs or images recur. Repetition can be a verbatim account of something that was previously stated, or it can be a variant in the form of a paraphrase or a close facsimile. Repeated material can be found immediately after the first time it occurs, or it can recall earlier sections of a text or narrative. Each of these types can serve a different purpose in a story, and we will see examples of all of them in our study of the encounter between Joseph and Pharaoh.

There is Repetition and There is Repetition (Qur'an 12:43-57)

The Qur'an's account of Joseph's release from prison is found in 12:43-57:

[43]The king said, "I saw in a dream seven fat cows being eaten by seven skinny ones, and seven green ears of corn along with seven others that were dry. Tell me what this means, nobles, if you are able to explain visions." [44]They said, "They were only confused nightmares. We do not know how to interpret dreams." [45]Then the one who had been freed remembered after all that time and said, "I will tell you its interpretation. Send me!" [46](He said) "Oh Joseph the truthful one, tell us the meaning of seven fat cows being eaten by seven skinny ones and seven green ears of corn along with seven others that are dry. Then I may return to the people and perhaps they will know." [47]He said, "Sow as you usually do for seven years. After you have harvested, leave the corn in the ears except for the small amount you will consume. [48]Then there will follow seven difficult years that will consume the grain you had stored up except for a little bit that will remain. [49]Then there will be a year of abundant rain when people will press grapes."

⁵⁰The king said, "Bring him to me!" When the messenger came to him, Joseph said, "Return to your master and ask him about the women who cut their hands. Truly, my Lord knows of their plots." ⁵¹He (the king) asked, "What is this about your trying to entice Joseph?" They replied, "Allah preserve us! We know no evil against him." The master's wife then said, "The truth is evident. I tried to seduce him but he is trustworthy." ⁵²(Joseph said) "May he know that I did not betray him while he was away. Truly, Allah does not guide the plots of those who betray. ⁵³I do not wish to absolve myself, because the soul tends toward evil unless my Lord shows mercy. Truly, my Lord is forgiving and merciful."

⁵⁴The king said, "Bring him to me so that I might choose him as a special assistant for myself." When he had spoken with him he said, "Today you have a secured and trusted position with us." ⁵⁵Joseph said, "Place me over the granaries of the land. I am an intelligent custodian." ⁵⁶Thus, We established Joseph in the land and he lived there as he pleased. We bestow Our mercy on whomever We wish and We do not waste the reward of the good. ⁵⁷The final reward is better for those who believe and obey.

In places this passage is marked by the same lack of narrative flow that was discussed in the previous chapter. The relationships among the events in the section are not always entirely clear, and there are certain gaps in the text that make it difficult for the reader to follow the chronological sequence. For example, why does the prisoner who was freed go to Joseph himself instead of telling the king about him? Does he hope to take credit for the interpretation Joseph will give him? Another question concerns how the king finds out about Joseph and his ability to interpret dreams. In v. 50 he commands that Joseph be brought into his presence, but the narrative does not indicate how he first hears about Joseph. Presumably the servant tells the king about him, but this scene is not described. A further mystery centers on Joseph's reluctance to leave prison until the matter of the ladies with the cut hands is resolved. Why does he bring this up now? There may be a good reason why Joseph raises the issue, but the reader must infer it from the text since it is never clearly stated.

The reference to the king's dreams that opens the section immediately calls to mind the dreams of Joseph (v. 4) and his fellow prisoners (v. 36) that have already been mentioned in the Qurʾan. The connection with the dreams of the prisoners is particularly strong because the reports of their dreams and that of the king all begin with the Arabic phrase *innī arā*, which translates literally as "I see." The beginning of Joseph's dream report is etymologically related to these others because he makes use of the perfect tense of the same Arabic verb and his words translate as "I saw" *(innī raʾaitu)*.

The opening of the passage also makes use of repetition in order to establish a link with Joseph's interpretive powers. When the king requests that his nobles tell him the meaning of his dream (v. 43), he uses a verb *(aftā)* that has the meaning "to explain." In the next verse the nobles admit their inability to explain by using a word *(taʾwīl)* best translated as "interpretation"; it will also be used by the released prisoner in v. 45. This is the same term that has already been used several times in connection with Joseph's ability to interpret dreams (vv. 6, 21, 36, 37). The repetition of this term sets the stage for Joseph's release. By using the word that describes Joseph's interpretive abilities *(taʾwīl)* the nobles are highlighting the fact that they are incapable of doing what he can do. Similarly, when the released prisoner asks to be sent so that he might be able to tell the king the *taʾwīl* of the dream, the reader knows he can only be going one place—to Joseph, the only character with whom the power of interpretation has been associated. The repetition of the word is a clue to the reader that Joseph is the only person who can tell the king the meaning of his dream.

There is an interesting grammatical problem in the released prisoner's request to the king in v. 45 when he says, "I will tell you its interpretation. Send me!" The Arabic pronominal suffix that is translated here as "its" can also be rendered "his." This ambiguity leaves open the possibility that the pronoun might be referring to Joseph and the man is therefore asking the king that he be sent to visit Joseph in prison. An argument in favor of this reading is the fact that these words come immediately after the text says that the man finally remembered Joseph after having forgotten him for years. Given the Qurʾan's tendency not to include all the elements of a narrative, it is conceivable that there is a gap in the text at this point: we are missing the description of the man's conversation with the king about what happened to him in prison. The narrative then picks up again after that point with the man asking to be sent to get "his" (Joseph's) interpretation.

There are some examples of verbatim repetition in the Qurʾan account. The first is when the released prisoner describes the king's dream to Joseph in the very same words the king himself used to describe it to his nobles (vv. 43 and 46). The verbatim nature of the retelling contrasts with what is found in Genesis, and this difference will be discussed below. For now it is sufficient to note that the identical form of the two reports puts Joseph in a position of authority vis-à-vis the king's nobles. Both he and they are presented with the very same dream, but only Joseph is able to discern its meaning. In other words, it is an illustration of the fact that he possesses the power they have already admitted is beyond their capability (v. 44).

Another example of verbatim repetition recalls a scene that was related somewhat earlier in the Qurʾan's Joseph story. The divine narrator's statement in v. 56, "Thus, We established Joseph in the land," is identical to what is found in v. 21 upon Joseph's arrival in the house of his Egyptian master and his wife. The link between the two verses is strengthened by the continuation of v. 21, which states that Allah taught Joseph the interpretation *(taʾwīl)* of events, using a word that is central to the present scene. The repetition of this phrase calls the reader's attention to Allah's ongoing presence and guidance in Joseph's life. Just as the deity was with him in the midst of the difficulty he encountered in his master's house, Allah will be with him now as he takes on the new responsibilities the king has entrusted to him.

The king repeats himself in v. 54, where the command "Bring him to me!" is the very same he uttered in v. 50. This order is not carried out the first time because Joseph sends the messenger back to the king to investigate the matter of the ladies. The second time the Egyptian ruler requests Joseph be brought to him the repetition is not verbatim because he adds a reason: "so that I might choose him as a special assistant for myself." This kind of augmentation of previously stated material is a fairly common form of repetition that can help to explain or highlight the meaning or intent of an earlier statement. That may be how it is functioning in this case as the king articulates the reason why he asked for Joseph in the first place.

More likely, however, the king's use of augmented repetition serves a different purpose in this passage. It appears to be a way of expressing his growing awareness of Joseph's true identity. The first time he says "Bring him to me!" comes right after Joseph gives his interpretation of the dream to the messenger. The Qurʾan does not report the messenger's return and communication of that interpretation to the king, but this appears to be the course of events since the man returns to Joseph later in v. 50. Upon hearing the interpretation, the king is still not sure what to make of Joseph and does not know if he should believe his explanation of the dream. So he commands the messenger to bring Joseph to him so that he might see him for himself and question him.

The second time the king requests that Joseph be brought to him he says that he wishes to take him on as an assistant. This is an unusual expansion of his earlier request that takes the reader by surprise. Why is the king now ready to hire Joseph, a man he has not yet met, who refused to come to him the first time he was summoned? The answer to that question lies in what happens between the two commands. Joseph refuses to come until the Egyptian investigates the circumstances surrounding his earlier encounter with the women. The king questions the ladies and discovers that Joseph is innocent of the charges leveled against him, and the master's wife even describes him as "trustworthy."

The king's opinion of Joseph undergoes a dramatic shift in the space of just three verses. In v. 50 he considers Joseph nothing more than a common criminal who might possess the uncommon power to interpret dreams, so he wants to see him in order to size him up for himself. After he listens to the women, his view of Joseph improves considerably. He now deems him to be a good man who is trustworthy and free of evil (v. 51). He also thinks that Joseph is someone he would like to have around on a permanent basis, and so he decides to hire him on the spot, sight unseen. This shift in the king's attitude toward Joseph is subtly indicated by the use of augmented repetition.

Unlike the Bible, the Qurʾan does not contain an extended dialogue between Joseph and the Egyptian ruler. In fact, each party speaks only one line to the other (vv. 54-55). Because the messenger acts as a go-between, the king never relates his dream directly to Joseph, and Joseph does not offer his interpretation in the king's presence. Nonetheless, the Islamic text does indicate, in v. 54, that the two did engage in conversation: "When he had spoken with him. . . ." But what did the two say to each other and how long did they speak? Narrated time is certainly longer than narration time for these six words (two in the original Arabic), but the reader is not privy to the content of their exchange and only knows the result of the conversation: the king decided to give Joseph a position of authority.

The text's reticence regarding what takes place between Joseph and the king raises an interesting question: What exactly does the Egyptian know about Joseph? The reader assumes that the messenger has given the king a full report the two times he returns from visiting Joseph in prison, but the Qurʾan does not say this explicitly. As already noted, Joseph's interpretation of the dream is never repeated to the king, either by the messenger or by Joseph himself, at any point in the story. The reader is more confident that the messenger has communicated Joseph's words to the king after the second trip because the king goes on to quiz the women about the very matter Joseph spoke of with the messenger in prison (vv. 50-51).

But what about Joseph's words in vv. 52-53? Has the king heard this statement, which is heavily theological and expresses Joseph's belief and trust in Allah? The text does not indicate to whom these words are spoken. If the king has heard them, this might explain why he is so quick to hire Joseph as his assistant: he sees him as a man of faith and integrity who can be trusted. Regardless of their intended audience, Joseph's comments here qualify as a type of repetition since they recall the mini-sermon he gave to his fellow prisoners in the previous section (vv. 37b-40). While the two speeches are not identical, they strike similar chords with their emphasis on Allah's role in human affairs. This is a good example of how even a subtle form of repetition that is more like an echo can contribute to characterization in a narrative. Having Joseph speak of his faith in a variety of different contexts is a way of affirming the reader's image of him as a spokesman for Allah who is unafraid to speak the truth in any situation.

The same type of repetition can be seen in the references to the ladies in v. 51 that recall the woman's attempted seduction of Joseph and the subsequent dinner party. This verse does not actually re-create those earlier scenes or quote verbatim from them, but it contains clear allusions to them that cause the reader to think back to them and remember Joseph's innocence, an idea that is central to the present passage. The link to the seduction and dinner scenes is also established through the double mention of the word "plots" (vv. 50 and 53). This repeats a theme we have seen to be a recurring one throughout the Qurʾan's Joseph story; it is particularly important in the scenes with the women (vv. 28, 33, 34).

It might also be said that Joseph's recognition of his own sinfulness in v. 53 ("I do not wish to absolve myself, because the soul tends toward evil unless my Lord shows mercy.") points back to his earlier encounters with the women. When his master's wife tries to entice him, it is said that he would have given in to her if Allah had not turned back evil and immorality from him (v. 24). Similarly, at the dinner party he admits his weakness and prays that Allah come to his assistance so he does not succumb to the women (v. 33). His acknowledgment of weakness here is in keeping with the image of his character that was established earlier and causes the reader to think back to the earlier episodes.

Joseph's reference to "my Lord" in v. 53 recalls the discussion of vv. 23 and 24, where a certain ambiguity was identified in his prior use of the term "lord." The context of the earlier passage suggested that he was referring to Allah, rather than his Egyptian master, with this designation, but an argument could be made for seeing the Egyptian as the referent the first time he uses the word in v. 23.

The reader confronts a similar situation in the present scene, since it is not immediately apparent who Joseph's "lord" is. His first use of the term is in v. 50 when, after asking the messenger to have the king inquire about the women, he says, "Truly, my Lord knows of their plots." Is Joseph speaking of the king or the deity? We cannot know with certainty, but there are at least two clues that point in the direction of the latter alternative. First of all, in the earlier scene when Joseph prays to Allah for help in overcoming the temptations of the women it is stated that his Lord, the one who knows, turned back their plots (v. 34). This is an argument in favor of identifying Allah as the Lord who knows their plots in v. 50.

A second reason has to do with Joseph's words in v. 50 just before his reference to his Lord: "Return to your master and ask him about the women who cut their hands." The Arabic word for master *(rabb)* is identical to the word translated "Lord" in the same verse. If Joseph wished to refer to the same individual (the Egyptian king) in both cases, it is unlikely that he would use an awkward construction that identifies him first as "your master" and then as "my master." More probably he would have maintained consistency and referred to him as "your master" both times or "he" the second time ("Return to your master and ask him about the women who cut their hands. Truly, *he/your master* knows of their plots").

It appears that Joseph is setting up a distinction in the verse between his Lord and the servant's master. If the latter knew of the women's plots, he would not have to ask them about their actions in order to get at the truth. But he is forced to interrogate them because he does not know what happened. Joseph's Lord, on the other hand, is the one who knows and, consequently, does not need to conduct an investigation. Allah's identity as Joseph's Lord is established beyond a shadow of a doubt in v. 53, which refers to powers and activities reserved only for the deity. "I do not wish to absolve myself, because the soul tends toward evil unless my Lord shows mercy. Truly, my Lord is forgiving and merciful."

In effect the reader, like the king, learns the identity of Joseph's Lord in stages. In v. 50 the repetition of the same term in reference to both the king and the deity muddies the water and creates ambiguity. Are Joseph's Lord and the servant's master one and the same? Three verses later the reader knows that this is impossible, because Joseph answers to a much higher power.

The text's attempt to bring the reader to a gradual awareness of Joseph's true identity is also discernible through another form of repetition found in the narrative. It is not always apparent in the English translation, but four times in this section a different character uses one or more titles in reference to Joseph that are meant to identify particular qualities or traits he possesses. The first example is found on the lips of the messenger when he calls Joseph "the truthful one" (v. 46). The woman who attempted to seduce him then refers to him as "one of the trustworthy" in v. 51, using an Arabic word *(ṣādiq)* that is etymologically related to the one used by the messenger *(ṣiddīq)*. The third instance is found in the king's words in v. 54, translated "Today you have a secured and trusted position with us." A more literal translation would render the sentence "Today you are a steadfast one and a trusted one before us." Finally, Joseph describes himself to the king as "an intelligent custodian" in v. 55. This last title is particularly revealing in that the word translated "intelligent" comes from the Arabic root related to knowledge *(ʿalima)*, which appears with great frequency throughout the course of the Qurʾan's Joseph story. In fact, this is the last of six occurrences of the root in the fourteen verses of this section of the story.

The presence of these titles throughout the passage keeps the reader's mind focused on the question of Joseph's identity. In this repetitive pattern each of the characters, including Joseph, contributes to the construction of a portrait that paints him in glowing terms. But the picture is not yet complete or reliable because the characters could be mistaken in their assessment of him. Verses 56 and 57 negate that possibility when the divine narrator states, "Thus, We established Joseph in the land and he lived there as he pleased. We bestow Our mercy on whomever We wish and We do not waste the reward of the good. The final reward is better for those who believe and obey." Allah provides the final titles that are beyond dispute and affirm the opinions of the other characters: Joseph is one of the good ones who believe and obey.

These final two verses of the section in the Qurʾan emphasize the role Allah has played in securing Joseph and clearing his good name. This continues a theme we have noted frequently in the Islamic text's telling of Joseph's story: Allah, rather than any human being, is responsible for Joseph's success and good fortune. In the present case, while it appears that the king is the one who frees Joseph and gives him a position of authority, it is actually Allah who does so. This idea is effectively conveyed through a final example of repetition that deserves comment. When Allah says "We established Joseph in the land" in v. 57, the verb used in the sentence *(makannā)* comes from the same Arabic root used by the king two verses earlier to describe Joseph's role as a special assistant who is secured, literally "a steadfast one" *(makīn).* The use of this root so soon after its initial occurrence causes the reader to think back to its first appearance and understand that Allah is actually the one who confers on Joseph the title that was first mentioned by the king.

Our analysis has shown that most of the repetition present in this section of the Qurʾan story serves to develop and enhance Joseph's character. Whether it is in the form of verbatim repetition, augmented repetition, paraphrase, reuse of the same Arabic word or root, or allusion that recalls previous episodes in the story, repetition is used to tell the reader something about Joseph and the privileged relationship he enjoys with Allah. In other words, in the encounter between Joseph and Pharaoh in the Qurʾan, Joseph is the focal point, and the use of repetition helps to underscore that fact. As we will now see, the same technique is used in Genesis to realize a completely different goal.

While the Qurʾan's description of Joseph's meeting with Pharaoh focuses on Joseph's character and his relationship with God, the biblical account highlights Pharaoh and what the deity will do for him. As usual, Genesis offers a tighter and more detailed version of the events, and it is also structured somewhat differently. This is most clearly seen when we consider how the three principal characters share the stage in the two books.

The released prisoner plays an important role in the Islamic text as an emissary who shuttles back and forth between Joseph and the king, communicating messages from one to the other. The actual encounter between Joseph and the king is described in a mere two verses in the Qurʾan, where each man has only one line of dialogue. In the biblical account, on the other hand, Joseph and the released prisoner never speak to one another, while the meeting between Pharaoh and Joseph is in the form of an extended conversation that covers thirty-two verses.

As in the Qurʾan, repetition is used throughout the biblical passage in order to call the reader's attention to certain elements in the text and to reiterate key themes. Unlike the Qurʾan, Genesis relies less on verbatim repetition and tends to tell a slightly different version the second time something is recounted. A comparison of how these different types of repetition function in the two stories can give us a good sense of the various ways this literary device can function in texts. Because of its length, we will consider the biblical material in two sections, the first treating events that lead up to Joseph's release (41:1-13) and the second describing his meeting with Pharaoh and his ascent to a position of authority in the Egyptian ruler's court (41:14-45).

Remembrance of Things Past (Genesis 41:1-13)

¹After two whole years, Pharaoh dreamed that he was standing by the Nile, ²and there came up out of the Nile seven sleek and fat cows, and they grazed in the reed grass. ³Then seven other cows, ugly and thin, came up out of the Nile after them, and stood by the other cows on the bank of the Nile. ⁴The ugly and thin cows ate up the seven sleek and fat cows. And Pharaoh awoke. ⁵Then he fell asleep and dreamed a second time; seven ears of grain, plump and good, were growing on one stalk. ⁶Then seven ears, thin and blighted by the east wind, sprouted after them. ⁷The thin ears swallowed up the seven plump and full ears. Pharaoh awoke, and it was a dream. ⁸In the morning his spirit was troubled; so he sent and called for all the magicians of Egypt and all its wise men. Pharaoh told them his dreams, but there was no one who could interpret them to Pharaoh.

⁹Then the chief cupbearer said to Pharaoh, "I remember my faults today. ¹⁰Once Pharaoh was angry with his servants, and put me and the chief baker in custody in the house of the captain of the guard. ¹¹We dreamed on the same night, he and I, each having a dream with its own meaning. ¹²A young Hebrew was there with us, a servant of the guard. When we told him, he interpreted our dreams to us, giving an

interpretation to each according to his dream. [13]As he interpreted to us, so it turned out; I was restored to my office, and the baker was hanged."

The references to dreams and their interpretations establish a link with early sections of the story where these items are important elements of the plot. The repeated use of this motif is more apparent in Genesis because Pharaoh has two dreams there, whereas he has only one in the Qurʾan. This continues the biblical pattern of double dreams that was also noted with Joseph (37:5-11) and the two prisoners (40:1-15). The pattern is not as neat in the Qurʾan, since Joseph has only one dream (v. 4) and the same thing appears to be true of Pharaoh (v. 43).

The content of Pharaoh's dreams in the Bible also makes use of a fuller type of repetition than what is found in the Qurʾan. In the Islamic version the elements of the vision are seven fat cows being eaten by seven skinny ones, and seven green ears of corn along with seven others that are dry. Both sets share the number seven, and both mention one group that is healthy and another that is less healthy. But there is no equivalent in the second set to the skinny cows eating the fat ones. The Genesis version further strengthens the connection between the two visions by having the thin and blighted ears of grain perform the same act as the ugly and thin cows when they devour the plump and full ears. Therefore the biblical text is more consistent and complete in its use of repetition in its description of Pharaoh's two dreams.

The cupbearer's words in vv. 11-13 match very closely what had been reported in 40:1-8 when he and the baker were placed in prison and told their dreams to Joseph. Except for a few changes necessitated by the fact that this is a first-person account of the events, virtually every word found in the Hebrew text of these three verses is also found in the earlier section. But it is not an example of verbatim repetition because it is a more abbreviated report of the happenings than what is contained in ch. 40. One of the most important omissions is that the cupbearer neglects to mention Joseph's words in 40:8: "Do not interpretations belong to God?" More than a simple oversight on the man's part, the absence of this question suggests that either the cupbearer forgot these words that Joseph spoke to him two years earlier or he did not understand their meaning at the time. We will see that Joseph goes to great lengths in ch. 41 to remind him, and Pharaoh, of the importance of what he had said in ch. 40.

When the cupbearer states three times in 41:12-13 that Joseph is the one who interpreted his and the baker's dreams, the reader immediately notes the discrepancy with Joseph's earlier comment that interpretations come from God. But Pharaoh lacks this knowledge, and his ignorance of the truth causes the reader to consider the scene from the Egyptian ruler's perspective. At this point he must rely solely on the cupbearer's inaccurate report of what happened in the prison two years earlier, and so he imagines Joseph to be some kind of magician or wise man similar to his own but possessing powers beyond theirs. He is still unaware of the source of Joseph's abilities, but once he has the opportunity to meet him face to face he will quickly learn why Joseph is able to interpret dreams.

The tendency to read the scene from Pharaoh's perspective is also strengthened by the use of repetition. In the description of his dreams the particle *hinneh* is found six times (vv. 1, 2, 3, 5, 6, 7) in the Hebrew text. It conveys the same meaning as the English word "behold," but it is often left out of translations of the Bible. Whenever it is found in biblical narrative the word places the reader in a character's position, and its repeated use here enables one to see the dreams as Pharaoh himself experienced them ("Behold! Seven sleek and fat cows. . . . Behold! Seven other cows . . ." etc.). The importance of this shift in perspective will become apparent as we now turn to the second section of the Genesis version of the events.

Anticipation of Things to Come (Genesis 41:14-45)

[14]Then Pharaoh sent for Joseph, and he was hurriedly brought out of the dungeon. When he had shaved himself and changed his clothes, he came in before Pharaoh. [15]And Pharaoh said to Joseph, "I have had a dream, and there is no one who can interpret it. I have heard it said of you that when you hear a dream you can interpret it." [16]Joseph answered Pharaoh, "It is not I; God will give Pharaoh a favorable answer." [17]Then Pharaoh said to Joseph, "In my dream I was standing on the banks of the Nile; [18]and seven cows, fat and sleek, came up out of the Nile and fed in the reed grass. [19]Then seven other cows came up after them, poor, very ugly, and thin. Never had I seen such ugly ones in all the land of Egypt. [20]The thin and ugly cows ate up the first seven fat cows, [21]but when they had eaten them no one would have known that they had done so, for they were still as ugly as before. Then I awoke. [22]I fell asleep a second time and I saw in my dream seven ears of grain, full and good, growing on one stalk, [23]and seven ears, withered, thin, and blighted by the east wind, sprouting after them; [24]and the thin ears swallowed up the seven good ears. But when I told it to the magicians, there was no one who could explain it to me."

[25]Then Joseph said to Pharaoh, "Pharaoh's dreams are one and the same; God has revealed to Pharaoh what he is about to do. [26]The seven good cows are seven years, and the seven good ears are seven years; the dreams are one. [27]The seven lean and ugly cows that came up after them are seven years, as are the seven empty ears blighted by the east wind. They are seven years of famine. [28]It is as I told Pharaoh;

God has shown to Pharaoh what he is about to do. [29]There will come seven years of great plenty throughout all the land of Egypt. [30]After them there will arise seven years of famine, and all the plenty will be forgotten in the land of Egypt; the famine will consume the land. [31]The plenty will no longer be known in the land because of the famine that will follow, for it will be very grievous. [32]And the doubling of Pharaoh's dream means that the thing is fixed by God, and God will shortly bring it about. [33]Now therefore let Pharaoh select a man who is discerning and wise, and set him over the land of Egypt. [34]Let Pharaoh proceed to appoint overseers over the land, and take one-fifth of the produce of the land of Egypt during the seven plenteous years. [35]Let them gather all the food of these good years that are coming, and lay up grain under the authority of Pharaoh for food in the cities, and let them keep it. [36]That food shall be a reserve for the land against the seven years of famine that are to befall the land of Egypt, so that the land may not perish through the famine."

[37]The proposal pleased Pharaoh and all his servants. [38]Pharaoh said to his servants, "Can we find anyone else like this—one in whom is the spirit of God?" [39]So Pharaoh said to Joseph, "Since God has shown you all this, there is no one so discerning and wise as you. [40]You shall be over my house, and all my people shall order themselves as you command; only with regard to the throne will I be greater than you." [41]And Pharaoh said to Joseph, "See, I have set you over all the land of Egypt." [42]Removing his signet ring from his hand, Pharaoh put it on Joseph's hand; he arrayed him in garments of fine linen, and put a gold chain around his neck. [43]He had him ride in the chariot of his second-in-command; and they cried out in front of him, "Bow the knee!" Thus he set him over all the land of Egypt. [44]Moreover Pharaoh said to Joseph, "I am Pharaoh, and without your consent no one shall lift up hand or foot in all the land of Egypt." [45]Pharaoh gave Joseph the name Zaphenath-paneah; and he gave him Asenath daughter of Potiphera, priest of On, as his wife. Thus Joseph gained authority over the land of Egypt.

Several aspects of this section recall earlier scenes in the Genesis Joseph story through the repetition of motifs or words. Joseph's clothing is mentioned twice, first when he shaves and changes his clothes prior to his meeting with Pharaoh (v. 14), and again when the Egyptian leader dresses him in fine attire after he interprets the dreams (v. 42). This continues the biblical narrative's pattern of referring to Joseph's clothing at key moments when he undergoes a change of status (37:3, 33; 39:12-18). In v. 14 his new clothes signal his transition from the degrading confinement of prison to the liberating freedom of Pharaoh's court. Similarly, when he is arrayed in splendid garments and jewelry in v. 42 Joseph is transformed from a common criminal into the second most powerful figure in the land. The latter scene also conveys the idea that Joseph has ceased being a foreigner and has taken on an Egyptian identity. His new name and wife, along with his new wardrobe, give him a complete makeover and put his old life behind him, at least for the time being.

Joseph's words to Pharaoh in v. 16 ("It is not I; God will give Pharaoh a favorable answer") echo what he said to his fellow prisoners in 40:8 ("Do not interpretations belong to God?"). It is not in the form of verbatim repetition, but the connection to the earlier scene presents the reader with a consistent view of Joseph's character and what he understands God's role in the interpretation of dreams to be. We will see that this is also the first of several references to God that will be repeated throughout the remainder of this section of the story.

This scene also repeats the familiar pattern of Joseph overcoming difficult circumstances and being put in a position of power by someone who recognizes his exceptional personal traits. Previously both Potiphar and the chief jailer made Joseph their second in command and invested him with much of their own authority. Now it is Pharaoh himself, authority personified in Egypt, who promotes Joseph and gives him the lofty title of vice-regent of the land. This promotion is reported in a way that leaves a bigger impression on the reader. The first two times the narrator simply states that Potiphar and the chief jailer place Joseph in a position of authority. But here Pharaoh's actual words to Joseph are reported in several places (vv. 38-41, 44), allowing the reader to hear of the promotion straight from the ruler's mouth. This has the effect of elevating Joseph even higher in the reader's mind. Joseph's new status is not communicated by means of an indirect report from the narrator that keeps the reader off the scene. The reader is able to hear the words of the most powerful person in the land as he turns over some of his authority to Joseph, the former slave and prisoner.

Quoting Pharaoh's words in direct discourse also allows the author to highlight a profound theological point that has been made throughout the course of the Genesis story. Pharaoh promotes Joseph for the same reason Potiphar and the chief jailer did: God is with Joseph. But unlike the other two, Pharaoh in v. 38 explicitly states that this is the reason: "Can we find anyone else like this—one in whom is the spirit of God?" Neither Potiphar nor the chief jailer ever makes a similar statement and, as already noted, it could be argued that the chief jailer is never even aware of the fact that the Lord is with Joseph.

The great king of Egypt, considered to be a god by his people, acknowledges the power and authority of Joseph's God. While Genesis does not explain how it is that Potiphar and the chief jailer come to know of

God's presence in Joseph's life, the text leaves no doubt regarding Pharaoh. It presents the reader with a step-by-step account of how Pharaoh is gradually made aware of who Joseph's God is, and it does so primarily through the use of repetition in the description of the dreams and Joseph's interpretation of them.

The first time the dreams are related (41:1-7) they are communicated by the narrator, an always reliable source whose report is accepted as an accurate description of what took place. The second time they are described (41:17-24), Pharaoh recalls his dreams and relates their contents to Joseph. But his recollection of the dreams does not agree with the narrator's account of them in all respects, because Pharaoh adds some elements that are not found in the initial dream report. Several of these additions are relatively unimportant and do not have a significant effect on the narrative. For example, in v. 19 Pharaoh adds the word "poor" to the adjectives "ugly" and "thin" that the narrator uses to describe the second set of cows in v. 3. He also refers to them as the ugliest cows he has ever seen (v. 19), a statement that has no parallel in the narrator's description. Similarly, in his recollection of the first set of ears of grain Pharaoh replaces the adjective "plump" with "full" (vv. 5, 22). He also adds the adjective "withered" to his description of the second set of ears (v. 23).

These are minor changes that have little bearing on how the text is read and understood. But there is another addition that is more significant and helps to explain how the plot develops in Genesis. In v. 21 Pharaoh says of the second set of cows, "but when they had eaten them no one would have known that they had done so, for they were still as ugly as before." The narrator's report of the dreams makes no mention of this detail, and its presence in Pharaoh's recollection of what he dreamt merits careful consideration.

From the structural point of view the introduction of this element disrupts the symmetry that is evident in the initial report of the dreams. The narrator describes two dreams that mirror each other very closely, as the following chart indicates.

Genesis 41:2-4	Genesis 41:5-7
Seven cows	Seven ears of grain
Seven other cows	Seven other ears of grain
Two adjectives for each group	Two adjectives for each group
Second group devours first group	Second group devours first group

Pharaoh's report of the dreams does not follow this pattern, because the material he adds on one side of the chart does not have a corresponding partner on the other side. In other words, the symmetry present in the narrator's description of the dreams is not found in Pharaoh's retelling. We can see this when we note the number of adjectives used to describe the two groups in each dream: the first group has two descriptors while the second group has three. Similarly, Pharaoh's comment that he had never seen such ugly cows (v. 19) has no equivalent in his report of the second dream.

The most significant addition is Pharaoh's remark in v. 21 that no one would have known the second group of cows ate the first group because they were still as ugly as before. His description of the second dream does not have a similar statement regarding the ears of grain. This, too, disrupts the overall symmetry of the dream account, but its real importance lies in its impact on the subsequent development of the plot.

When we note this discrepancy in how Pharaoh and the narrator report the dreams we must assume the latter's account is correct, because the biblical narrator is always reliable and trustworthy. This means that Pharaoh did not remember his dreams correctly, and he communicated an inaccurate description of them to Joseph and, presumably, to his magicians and wise men. This explains why the members of Pharaoh's court were unable to interpret his dreams: they had received a distorted version of his visions and were not able to make sense of them. In this case the lack of verbatim repetition when the dreams are reiterated leads to a complication in the plot that requires a resolution in the form of Joseph's release from prison.

When the magicians and wise men listen to Pharaoh's erroneous description of his dreams they are unable to recognize that the two dreams are communicating the same message. In particular, his comment in v. 21 that one would not have known that the second set of cows had eaten the first because they were still ugly breaks the connection between the two dreams and causes the magicians to think of them as two separate and discrete visions. This is what makes Joseph's correct interpretation all the more remarkable. He hears the same dream report as the others, but he is able to discern that Pharaoh's dreams are "one and the same" (v. 25). This establishes Joseph's superiority over Pharaoh and his wise men as someone who is able to correctly interpret the divine will even when the dreams through which it is revealed are not accurately recalled.

This is a good example of the important role repetition can play in biblical narrative. If the text had simply said that Pharaoh told Joseph his dreams without providing his exact words, the reader would logically assume that the reports of the narrator and the Egyptian were identical. By repeating the content of the dreams and making some subtle changes in the way the dreams are repeated the author is able to influence the reader's view of the characters in the story.

Another example of this can be seen in Joseph's use of repetition in his interpretation of Pharaoh's dreams. It has already been noted that in 41:16 he identifies God as the one who ultimately holds the power to interpret. He picks up on this theme when he makes reference to God's involvement three other times in the course of his conversation with Pharaoh. After the ruler relates the contents of his dreams to him, Joseph says in v. 25, "God has revealed to Pharaoh what he is about to do." With these words Joseph informs Pharaoh right away that his dreams are a message from God. Joseph makes the same point in v. 28 when he says, "It is as I told Pharaoh; God has shown to Pharaoh what he is about to do." The final mention of God is found in v. 33 where Joseph informs the Egyptian, "And the doubling of Pharaoh's dream means that the thing is fixed by God, and God will shortly bring it about."

The repetition is not verbatim, but the message is the same: God is the one who has caused Pharaoh to have these dreams, and with God's help Joseph can tell Pharaoh what they mean. This refrain, found four times in Joseph's conversation with the Egyptian ruler, is repeated so frequently because Joseph wants to be certain that Pharaoh is aware of the source of the dreams and their interpretation. He is not like Pharaoh's magicians and wise men, who are able to discern the meaning of dreams on their own. Joseph is totally dependent upon God's power and presence if he is going to be able to shed light on the significance of the dreams.

Joseph's repetition of this idea does the trick, and the message sinks in. Throughout Joseph's explanation of the dreams' meaning, a section that runs twelve verses, Pharaoh never says a word. The reader wonders whether the great leader of Egypt, considered a god by his people, will be receptive to the message this recently-released foreign prisoner is communicating to him. His very first words in vv. 38 and 39 convincingly resolve the matter. "Can we find anyone else like this—one in whom is the spirit of God? . . . Since God has shown you all this, there is no one as discerning and wise as you." Joseph's persistence in repeatedly reminding Pharaoh of God's involvement pays off as the Egyptian utters a statement that acknowledges the authority and power of Joseph's God.

It is interesting to compare this scene to its counterpart in the Qur'an. The Islamic text does not report an extensive conversation between Joseph and the Egyptian king. Each party speaks only one line of dialogue to the other, and God is not mentioned by either. One would have to read into the text or between the lines in order to reach the conclusion that the king knows God is with Joseph. The Bible reader is more certain of this fact because

Pharaoh himself says as much. He is able to acknowledge God's role in the Genesis narrative because of the effective way repetition is used to reinforce the point and gradually bring him to an awareness of the truth. Ironically, then, the theme of knowledge that is so central to the Qurʾan's version of the Joseph story is not as apparent in its scene between Joseph and Pharaoh as it is in the Bible's.

It might be better to say that knowledge is a critical component of both texts but is used to achieve a different purpose in each. In the Islamic tradition it is knowledge of Joseph and his role that is primary in the narrative. Repetition is used to assert his innocence and to highlight the close relationship he has with Allah. But it is primarily the reader who is the beneficiary of this knowledge, since the text does not explicitly indicate that the king is made aware of this information. Certainly the king and the other characters recognize Joseph to be an exceptional person, but their perception of Allah's presence in his life is less clear.

This is apparent when we recall that four times throughout the Qurʾan's version titles are used to describe Joseph, thereby keeping the focus of the text on his identity and situation. We find no such titles referring to Joseph in Genesis, other than the cupbearer's description of him as a "young Hebrew" (v. 12). In fact, even though he is called by his name throughout the biblical account, it could be said that "Joseph" ceases to exist because Pharaoh gives him an Egyptian name (v. 46). The focus in Genesis is on God, not Joseph. The deity is mentioned four times in the important scene that has Joseph interpret Pharaoh's dreams. When Pharaoh does speak of Joseph's identity, he stresses the role of God in his life: Joseph is the one in whom is the spirit of God, and God has shown him all this.

Knowledge of God and what God will do for Pharaoh and Egypt is a central theme of the Genesis scene. Joseph rises in stature to the point that he is the second most powerful person in all the land. But God rises in stature more, and Joseph's success is contingent upon Pharaoh's acknowledging the authority of God. His ability to do so is due in no small part to the way repetition functions in the text.

CHAPTER FIVE

Gaps: Joseph and His Brothers (Genesis 42:1–44:17; Qur'an 12:58-86)

A question that commonly crosses the mind of any reader is "Where is all this heading?" As the events of a narrative unfold and the structure of its plot begins to take shape, it is natural for the reader to reflect on the possible directions the story might take. One of the most engaging aspects of the reading experience is found in this attempt to anticipate plot developments and predict how a story will end.

The Joseph story is no different. When he is sold by his brothers and arrives in Egypt, the question begins to surface over and over again in the reader's mind: "Where is all this heading?" What will happen to Joseph in Egypt? Will Potiphar's wife successfully seduce him? Will he get out of prison? If so, how and when? Even if they are not explicitly articulated, these and similar questions inevitably arise in the course of reading the narrative.

The repetition of the theme of Joseph's success despite difficult circumstances and his promotion to a position of authority subtly reinforces this questioning mode. Three different times Joseph proves that it is impossible to keep him down. Each time he finds himself in a trying situation the reader wonders what the outcome will be. Will Joseph continue to thrive, or has his string of luck run out, preventing him from advancing any further? When Joseph is named second in command in Egypt the reader wonders what he can possibly do for an encore. Short of taking the throne himself, it appears that Joseph has climbed as high as he can on the ladder to success.

But the narrative still has some unfinished business. This is not just the story of a foreigner who thrives in his new surroundings. It is also the story of someone who has been rejected by those closest to him and is forced to leave his home. From the moment Joseph lands in the well, the possibility of a future family reunion continues to bubble just under the surface of the text. Will Joseph ever see his brothers again? The interpretations of his two dreams (37:5-11) that have them bowing down to him suggest that such a meeting will take place. But the reader does not know when or how it will happen. Then a clue is dropped. As Joseph stands at the pinnacle of his power, as far from the bottom of a well as a person can be, the biblical narrator slyly hints at the upcoming events that will complicate his life. "Moreover, all the world came to Joseph in Egypt to buy grain, because the famine became severe throughout the world" (41:57).

Among those flocking to Egypt will be Joseph's brothers, and both the Bible and the Qurʾan present this family gathering as a dramatic high point of the story. As is usually the case, the Islamic version is a model of brevity while the Genesis account is more elaborate and detailed. In fact, nowhere else in the entire story is this difference more pronounced than here: what the Qurʾan describes in 28 verses takes 88 in Genesis. This is primarily due to the presence in the Bible of several episodes that have no counterparts in the Qurʾan, resulting in a text that extends the action and keeps the reader waiting longer to see "where all this is heading."

This chapter will consider an aspect of the narratives that complicates the reader's attempt to anticipate how the story will end. Both texts make use of a literary device known as "gapping" that piques the reader's curiosity while adding ambiguity to the plot. It refers to the author's decision to leave out certain things from a story, particularly elements whose absence raises questions for the reader regarding the characters and events of a narrative. In other words, we will be paying attention to the holes in the text. We have already noted a number of gaps in the Genesis version of the story. What is going through Joseph's mind while he is in the pit? How close does he come to giving in to the advances of Potiphar's wife? Why did the cupbearer forget to mention Joseph to Pharaoh? Such questions cannot be resolved with certainty because the reader does not have enough information to answer them.

What is not present in a text can play as important a role in the reading process as what is present. Gaps that limit knowledge can call the reader's attention to certain aspects of a narrative and draw him or her into the story in a way that would not be possible if all the information had been provided. Mysteries and suspense novels are built on this premise. The typical "whodunit" is structured in a way that limits the reader's knowledge by withholding certain information and doling out the rest a little at a time. In the process, the reader gets caught up in the action and tries to solve the mystery based on the information he or she has.

While not a mystery in the usual sense of the word, the Joseph story has an element of the mysterious that will be explored in this chapter. Perhaps the biggest unknown is what will happen if Joseph and his brothers should be reunited. Even when they eventually find themselves together this question is not immediately answered. The reader, especially the Bible reader, must first go through a series of twists and turns in the narrative before the mystery is solved. In addition, the presence of gaps in the text creates an ambiguity that leaves the reader guessing about the outcome until the very last moment.

Gaps come in a variety of forms. Sometimes the details of something mentioned in the story are left out. For instance, it is stated in Gen 37:2 that Joseph brought Jacob a "bad report" about his brothers, but the content of that report is not given. Elsewhere chronological gaps make it impossible to know the narrative time of an event. We see an example of this in 39:20–40:3, where there is no way of knowing how long Joseph is in prison before the arrival of the cupbearer and chief baker. Some of the most intriguing gaps are those places in a narrative that are silent about what is going on inside a character's head. The lack of access to a character's thoughts or reactions leads to a high level of uncertainty and ambiguity for the reader. On occasion the narrator provides information about the mental state of characters. A good example of this is seen in 41:37 when, after Joseph interprets Pharaoh's dreams, it is said, "The proposal pleased Pharaoh and all his servants." Such a statement gives the reader an idea of the characters' state of mind and facilitates the process of anticipating what will come next. But at other times the narrator does not fill in the gap and the reader is forced to infer or read between the lines, never quite sure about what a character is thinking.

This is precisely the situation in the scene that describes Joseph's reunion with his brothers. The length of the Genesis version makes it impossible to include all of it, and so the format adopted in previous chapters will not be followed here. Rather, those sections that are most relevant for our purposes will be cited, and the rest will be summarized throughout the course of the discussion.

Opportunity, But No Motive

After being absent from the Genesis account since ch. 37, Joseph's brothers reappear in 42:1. With a few brief exceptions they will be in every scene throughout the next four chapters, a section covering 134 verses. Our analysis will treat the events of the narrative up until the speech of Judah that begins in 44:18 and leads to Joseph's disclosure of his true identity. Throughout this section Joseph says and does many things, but the narrator rarely takes the reader below the surface to give a sense of what is going on inside him. This means that the reader must rely solely on Joseph's actions and words in order to determine his reaction to the events and his motivation for behaving as he does. As we have noted previously, this approach is open to all kinds of problems and opportunities. Words and actions can be interpreted in many different ways, and characters do not always express outwardly what they are feeling within. This is clearly the case in this section, where Joseph's behavior is not easy to understand or analyze.

When Joseph's brothers arrive in Egypt looking for grain he sets them back on their heels by treating them gruffly and hurling accusations at them.

> [7]When Joseph saw his brothers, he recognized them, but he treated them like strangers and spoke harshly to them. "Where do you come from?" he said. They said, "From the land of Canaan, to buy food." [8]Although Joseph had recognized his brothers, they did not recognize him. [9]Joseph also remembered the dreams that he had dreamed about them. He said to them, "You are spies; you have come to see the nakedness of the land!" [10]They said to him, "No, my lord; your servants have come to buy food. [11]We are all sons of one man; we are honest men; your servants have never been spies." [12]But he said to them, "No, you have come to see the nakedness of the land!" [13]They said, "We, your servants, are twelve brothers, the sons of a certain man in the land of Canaan; the youngest, however, is now with our father, and one is no more." [14]But Joseph said to them, "It is just as I have said to you; you are spies! [15]Here is how you shall be tested: as Pharaoh lives, you shall not leave this place unless your youngest brother comes here! [16]Let one of you go and bring your brother, while the rest of you remain in prison, in order that your words may be tested, whether there is truth in you; or else, as Pharaoh lives, surely you are spies." [17]And he put them all together in prison for three days. (42:7-17)

The charge that they are spies is untrue, but it enables Joseph to prolong his brothers' stay in the land and delay their departure. It appears that he wants to make them squirm, and squirm they do. In the course of their defense they speak three times, each time revealing a little more about who they are. At first they are only Canaanites who have come to buy food (v. 7). Then they identify themselves as brothers, honest men who have never been spies (v. 11). Finally, they give him the family history complete with information on the two brothers who are not with them (v. 13). There is a marvelous sense of irony to the scene as the brothers come clean about who they are while Joseph stands before them, poker-faced, the missing piece that would complete the family portrait.

Joseph's treatment of them is understandable in light of what they did to him years ago, and it may be that he is enjoying this opportunity to give the brothers a taste of their own medicine. But the reader does not know for sure because Joseph's thoughts remain a mystery. What is his motivation for accusing them of being spies? What is his intention behind imprisoning them for three days? He may be motivated by revenge, but it might also be that his primary aim is to be reunited with Benjamin, his full brother. Perhaps it is a combination of factors that causes him to throw them in jail so they can experience what he went through in the pit and in his own prison cell. Or perhaps he is confused and is not sure exactly what his response to this unexpected visit from the past should be. That would explain why, after three days, he changes his mind about what to do with them.

> [18]On the third day Joseph said to them, "Do this and you will live, for I fear God: [19]if you are honest men, let one of your brothers stay here where you are imprisoned. The rest of you shall go and carry grain for the famine of your households, [20]and bring your youngest brother to me. Thus your words will be verified, and you shall not die." And they agreed to do so.

The reason for this change of plans is not stated. Maybe it is a purely practical decision meant to feed as many people as possible: nine brothers would be able to transport much more grain to Canaan than one. This would be a good faith gesture on Joseph's part meant to tell Jacob and the other family members that he is committed to their survival. On the other hand, maybe Joseph is more interested in his own welfare than that of his family. If only one brother returns and reports that the others are in prison and Joseph wants him to bring Benjamin to Egypt, it is highly unlikely that Jacob would agree to the request, out of fear that he would lose them all. If Joseph allows all but one to return, and loads them up with grain, the odds are better that Jacob would let Benjamin accompany them on a return trip to Egypt. Both scenarios are plausible, but the truth remains unknown since the narrator furnishes no clues regarding what is going on in Joseph's mind.

The second time he speaks to the brothers, Joseph's message undergoes a subtle shift that is equally difficult to interpret. Before placing them in prison he twice uses the phrase "as Pharaoh lives," calling on the Egyptian monarch as his witness (vv. 15, 16). Three days later he does not mention Pharaoh, but tells the brothers that he fears God (v. 18). Is this a strategic decision on Joseph's part? He might be referring to the deity and downplaying his loyalty to the Egyptian ruler in an effort to win over the brothers. Once again the reader is unable to answer the question, but the shift is an intriguing one.

Up to this point in the Genesis version Joseph's character is impenetrable. His words and actions are plainly described, but the motives and feelings behind them are unknown. Obviously he wants Benjamin to come to Egypt, but even the reason behind this desire is not stated. The reader has no way of knowing how this unexpected family reunion is affecting Joseph internally. Then a crack in his armor appears. In 42:21-22 the brothers discuss among themselves the cause of their current predicament, and their thoughts drift back to that day a long time ago when they sold Joseph. They conclude that they are now being paid back for the way they mistreated him. The narrator inserts a comment that adds to the drama of the moment. "They did not know that Joseph understood them, since he spoke with them through an interpreter."

As the brothers openly acknowledge their guilt regarding Joseph they are unaware of two facts: the Egyptian official before whom they now stand can understand every word they say, and he is none other than Joseph himself. What Joseph hears is more than he can bear, and it leads to an uncharacteristic show of emotion.

> [24]He turned away from them and wept; then he returned and spoke to them. And he picked out Simeon and had him bound before their eyes. [25]Joseph then gave orders to fill their bags with grain, to return every man's money to his sack, and to give them provisions for their journey. This was done for them.

The reader might be tempted to think that Joseph's crying is a sign that he is softening, but this would be to read too much into the text. In fact, his feelings and motivation still remain a mystery. The contrast between him and the brothers on this point is striking. As they pour out their souls and express remorse, perhaps for the first time, over an act they committed years ago, their emotions are raw and right on the surface. Joseph's thoughts, on the other hand, continue to be hidden from the reader, and his tears only make this more apparent. He cries because of something he is feeling, but what is it—anger, betrayal, love, or something else? The return of his brothers' money might be interpreted as an act of fraternal solidarity and support, but even this is ambiguous because Joseph might be doing it to achieve a sinister purpose that will only later become apparent. The reader continues to wait for a clear indication of Joseph's true state of mind.

Another gap in the text is revealed in what the brothers say in v. 21. "Alas, we are paying the penalty for what we did to our brother; we saw his anguish when he pleaded with us, but we would not listen." Chapter 37 makes no mention of a reaction from Joseph when his brothers get rid of him. Only now is that gap filled in as the reader is told that Joseph pleaded for his life with his brothers. Why the delay in reporting this significant detail? Perhaps the author has waited until now to disclose it so that the reader will more easily be able to identify with Joseph's character and see the events from his perspective. Just as Joseph experiences a flashback to this painful episode in his life, the reader is also brought back to it, but now with an added element that underscores the pain and distress that Joseph felt. This shows that gaps are not always permanent in a narrative and can sometimes be filled in at a later point to achieve a dramatic effect.

Joseph is off the scene for the next twenty-five verses or so as the brothers return to Jacob and the setting shifts to Canaan. This material will be treated below when we consider the other characters in the narrative. When the brothers, including Benjamin, go back to Egypt, Joseph quizzes them on family matters:

> [26]When Joseph came home, they brought him the present that they had carried into the house, and bowed to the ground before him. [27]He inquired about their welfare, and said, "Is your father well, the old man of whom you spoke? Is he still alive?" [28]They said, "Your servant our father is well; he is still alive." And they bowed their heads and did obeisance. [29]Then he looked up and saw his brother Benjamin, his mother's son, and said, "Is this your youngest brother, of whom you spoke to me? God be gracious to you, my son!" [30]With that, Joseph hurried out, because he was overcome with affection for his brother, and he was about to weep. So he went into a private room and wept there. [31]Then he washed his face and came out; and controlling himself he said, "Serve the meal." (43:26-31)

For the first time since his brothers arrived in Egypt the reader is given a glimpse into what is going on inside Joseph. In a scene reminiscent of the earlier one when Joseph cried after overhearing his brothers, he is once again forced to leave their presence, only this time the reason for his tears is plainly stated. He is "overcome with affection" for Benjamin and flees the room rather than break down in front of them. The reader now has some sense of Joseph's emotional state, but it is still only a partial knowledge. There is no doubt about his love for Benjamin, but what are his feelings toward the other brothers? The act of leaving the room is a telling one and might reflect a sense of uncertainty on his part about how to proceed. He is still unable to disclose his true identity to them and, for some reason, prefers to continue the charade a bit longer.

His questions about Jacob also shed indirect light on Joseph's thought process as he formulates a course of action. The brothers probably consider this to be nothing more than small talk or polite conversation after their trip from Canaan, but Joseph is inquiring about a matter of great importance for himself. If his father is alive, the family is still intact and a reunion between Joseph and Jacob would be possible. But if he has died, such a meeting cannot take place and the brothers are the only family left for Joseph. In the latter case he might prefer to keep his identity a secret from the brothers, especially if he still harbors ill will toward them for what they did to him years ago. But now that he knows Jacob is still alive, he will have to tell his brothers who he is if he wishes to see his father again.

The foregoing is nothing but a plausible reconstruction of the thoughts that Joseph might be having as he weighs his options and ponders his next move. The simple fact is that the reader is still clueless about everything except Joseph's affection for Benjamin. But this is no small matter since Joseph probably wants nothing more than to be able to reveal his true identity to his younger brother. A sense of the inner turmoil he is experiencing is communicated in the detail that he is still struggling to control himself as he returns to his brothers and orders that the meal be served (v. 31).

The mention of the meal is an unexpected twist in the plot that grabs the reader's attention. Given the nature of their relationship (at least as the brothers perceive it) it is most unusual that an Egyptian official would ask a group of foreigners to dine with him. What is the reason behind this invitation? A reasonable answer that comes to the reader's mind is that Joseph has decided to end the masquerade and tell his brothers who he is. What better setting to do so than at a meal? Once the food and wine have begun to do their work, Joseph can surprise the brothers with his news and turn the gathering into a celebratory banquet.

Such an outcome never materializes, but Joseph does use the meal to get the brothers (and the reader) wondering about what is going on.

> [33]When they were seated before him, the firstborn according to his birthright and the youngest according to his youth, the men looked at one another in amazement. [34]Portions were taken to them from Joseph's table, but Benjamin's portion was five times as much as any of theirs. So they drank and were merry with him. (43:33-34)

The unusual seating arrangement and super-sized portions for Benjamin can only be due to orders from the head table. It is as if Joseph has devised his own version of mystery dinner theater by leaving clues for the brothers that point to the identity of the host. Who else but their own brother would know their order of birth? Who else but Benjamin's own brother would want to give him an extra helping? The answer is right before their eyes, but the brothers miss the clues. The reader imagines that Joseph is enjoying this cat-and-mouse game immensely and expects him to remove his mask at any moment. The comment that the brothers were drinking and making merry with Joseph suggests a reunion is just around the corner.

But the mask stays on. The next thing we know, Joseph orders his steward to send the brothers on their way in a manner that echoes the last time they left his presence. "Fill the men's sacks with food, as much as they can carry, and put each man's money in the top of his sack. Put my cup, the silver cup, in the top of the sack of the youngest, with his money for the grain" (44:1a-2). Joseph's motivation for doing this is as mysterious as ever, but the addition of the silver cup this time indicates he has a plan in mind that will involve Benjamin's future.

In a scene that is both clever and devious, Joseph achieves his goal by toying with the brothers and getting them to indict themselves (44:4-13). The brothers do not get very far from the city when Joseph's steward overtakes them and confronts them about the missing cup. Certain of their collective innocence, they suggest a punishment if the cup should be found in their possession: the guilty party will be executed and the others will becomes the man's slaves. The steward proposes alternative terms in 44:10. "Even so; in accordance with your words, let it be: he with whom it is found shall become my slave, but the rest of you shall go free." Still convinced that they have nothing to hide, the brothers allow their bags to be searched and, performing the standard ritual that is enacted when one receives bad news, tear their clothing when the cup is found with Benjamin.

When they are brought back to Joseph, the brothers acknowledge their guilt and propose yet another form of punishment, one that he rejects in favor of that put forth by his steward.

> [16]And Judah said, "What can we say to my lord? What can we speak? How can we clear ourselves? God has found out the guilt of your servants; here we are then, my lord's slaves, both we and also the one in whose possession the cup has been found." [17]But he said, "Far be it from me that I should do so! Only the one in whose possession the cup was found shall be my slave; but as for you, go up in peace to your father." (44:16-17)

Throughout the scene the reader is not explicitly told anything about Joseph's thoughts and motivation, but a consideration of the steward's role in the narrative can help to fill in this gap. It is interesting that the alternative punishment the steward proposes to the brothers is the very one Joseph himself decides on when they come before him. In all probability Joseph let the steward know that this was his preference before sending him after the brothers. This is another piece of information that is not reported in the text, but the context of the story suggests it is the most logical reason why the steward rejects the brothers' suggestion. As Joseph's servant he is not in a position to determine the appropriate punishment for an offense, even a fictitious one, against his master. That would be Joseph's call. The fact that Joseph opts for the same punishment is an argument in favor of the steward's having been made aware of what Joseph wanted prior to going after the brothers.

This suggests that, all along, Joseph is primarily interested in finding a way to keep Benjamin with him in Egypt without blowing his own cover. Once again it should be pointed out that this is a plausible reconstruction of his motives and thoughts that must remain hypothetical because of the gaps in the reader's knowledge of what is going on inside Joseph. One can only get at what Joseph is thinking by reading between the lines and inferring from the information the narrative provides. The reading proposed here seems reasonable in light of Joseph's actions and the behavior and words of the other characters, especially the steward.

Compared to Joseph, the brothers' feelings and thoughts read like an open book. Throughout this section of the story the reader is given access to what they are thinking by way of comments from the narrator and statements the brothers make. But there are still a number of gaps that limit the reader's knowledge and add to the drama. For example, when Joseph accuses them of being spies and has them imprisoned (42:15-17), their reaction to this turn of events is not described. What goes through their minds during the three days they spend incarcerated? This establishes a further connection between their experience and that of Joseph when he is thrown into the well but his reaction is not reported.

On the other hand, we have seen that the brothers openly express their thoughts three days later when Joseph keeps Simeon and sends the others back home. They recall what they did to Joseph years ago and they consider their present predicament to be a punishment for the way they treated him (42:21-22). The reader has every reason to believe this is an accurate expression of what they are feeling because they do not know Joseph can understand them as they speak candidly and honestly among themselves.

In a number of places the brothers' emotional reaction to events is described. When they leave Egypt the first time, one of them opens his bag on the way home and makes a startling discovery.

27When one of them opened his sack to give his donkey fodder at the lodging place, he saw his money at the top of the sack. 28He said to his brothers, "My money has been put back; here it is in my sack!" At this they lost heart and turned trembling to one another, saying, "What is this that God has done to us?" (42:27-28)

They have a similar reaction a few verses later when, after arriving back in Canaan, they find the rest of the money. "As they were emptying their sacks, there in each one's sack was his bag of money. When they and their father saw their bundles of money, they were dismayed." This is a curious scene that points to another gap in the text: after the first brother found his money in his bag, why did the rest of them not immediately look to see if their money had been returned as well? The text does not answer this question, but it could be a way of prolonging the drama and drawing the reader into the story in anticipation of the rest of the discovery.

The brothers' anxiety is also mentioned in 43:18 when they are called to Joseph's house after returning to Egypt.

18Now the men were afraid because they were brought to Joseph's house, and they said, "It is because of the money, replaced in our sacks the first time, that we have been brought in, so that he may have an opportunity to fall upon us, to make slaves of us and take our donkeys."

The steward goes on to reassure them that they are not in any trouble and their money was received. Nonetheless, their statement and the narrator's comment that they were afraid indicate that they are near panic as they wait to meet with the Egyptian official. If it has been Joseph's intent to fill them with fear and uncertainty he has succeeded admirably. But, as we have noted, the reader has no way of knowing exactly what Joseph's intentions are because they are never revealed. The contrast between his character and the brothers on this point is striking. For the most part Joseph's thoughts and feelings are inaccessible, and his motives remain hidden from view. Conversely, the reader is told quite a bit about the brothers' reaction to their circumstances.

Quite a bit, but not everything: one of the most significant gaps for the reader concerns the brothers' insistence that they all become Joseph's slaves after the cup is found with Benjamin (44:9, 16). The first time they suggest this penalty they believe they are innocent of the charges, and so they are certain there will be no punishment. But after the cup is found in Benjamin's bag and they return to Joseph, they repeat their intention to become his slaves. Why do the brothers volunteer to spend the rest of their lives in servitude to Joseph, particularly when they know they did not take the cup and all fingers point to Benjamin as the guilty party?

There are at least two possible answers to this question. They may be concerned about the welcome they will receive if they should return to Canaan without Benjamin. Jacob's words in 42:38 show how adamantly opposed he was to the idea of Benjamin going back to Egypt with them. "My son shall not go down with you, for his brother is dead, and he alone is left. If harm should come to him on the journey that you are to make, you would bring down my gray hairs with sorrow to Sheol." Against his better judgment he allows them to take Benjamin after they convince him that Joseph will not give them any more food if they return without their youngest brother. As they now stand before the Egyptian official they might be imagining what could happen to Jacob, and to them, if they return home without Benjamin. With that unappealing prospect in mind they propose a sentence that requires they stay in Egypt.

A second possibility emerges from another gap in the text that has not yet been discussed. In 44:16 Judah speaks for the group when he says, "What can we say to my lord? What can we speak? How can we clear ourselves? God has found out the guilt of your servants." This confession of guilt is curious and unexpected since the brothers did not take the cup and, as far as they know, they have done nothing wrong to this Egyptian official. Are they trying to protect their little brother and, in a show of fraternal solidarity, admitting to a crime they did not commit?

Perhaps, but it is more likely that Judah is recalling another crime they did commit a long time ago that continues to haunt them. He interprets their present predicament in light of what they did to Joseph, and he believes they are now being punished for the way they mistreated him. The brothers' own comments a bit earlier in the story support this reading. When Joseph released them from prison after three days and allowed all but Simeon to return to Canaan, the brothers made the connection with their crime against Joseph (42:21). "Alas, we are paying the penalty for what we did to our brother; we saw his anguish when he pleaded with us, but we would not listen. That is why this anguish has come upon us." Judah and the rest of the brothers are guilty because of what happened in Dothan in ch. 37, not because of what happened in Egypt in ch. 44.

It took seven chapters of narration time and many years of narrated time, but the wheels of justice have finally caught up with them. The moment is rich with drama and irony because the brothers are unknowingly admitting their guilt to the very person they violated. This is such an effective scene because of the way gaps function within it. The entire plot is built around the brothers' lack of knowledge regarding who the Egyptian official really is. Joseph, in turn, has no idea about what is taking place in Canaan as the brothers shuttle back and forth and convince Jacob to allow Benjamin to come with them. The reader is privy to all this information but must deal with other gaps present in the narrative. Foremost among these are the thoughts and motivations of the characters, especially Joseph. Even as the brothers admit their guilt and another opportunity is presented for Joseph to reveal his true identity, the Bible reader has no idea where all this is headed.

Their Thoughts Are Not Our Thoughts (Qur²an 12:58-86)

It is even more difficult to discern the thoughts of Joseph and his family in the Qur²an. The Genesis version offers a few clues, however ambiguous, about the state of mind of the characters, but the Islamic text leaves the reader mostly guessing about their reactions and feelings. As we will see, the result is a story that does not engage or draw in the reader in quite the same way as the biblical account. The ambiguity inherent in Genesis (Why does Joseph weep? Why does he invite the brothers to a meal?) is a compelling aspect of the story that causes the reader to reflect on the motivations and thoughts of the characters in an attempt to determine where the plot might be headed. In other words, the ambiguity makes a positive contribution to the reading experience.

In contrast, the Qur²an version is often opaque rather than ambiguous: with rare exceptions, the characters' thoughts are off-limits to the reader and there are very few hints indicating what they might be. This difference comes out clearly when we compare the way the two texts describe the first meeting between Joseph and the brothers.

> [58]Then Joseph's brothers came. When they entered he recognized them but they did not recognize him. [59]When he had supplied them with their goods he said, "Bring your brother to me. Do you not see that I have given to you a full measure and that I am the best host? [60]If you do not bring him to me you will not receive another measure from me nor should you come near here again." [61]They answered, "We will make every effort to get him from his father." He said to his servants, "Put their goods back in their packs. Perhaps they will find them when they get home and perhaps they will return."

Many of the details in Genesis that cause the reader to wonder about the thoughts and motivations of the characters are not present in the Islamic version. The brothers do not bow down to Joseph, an act mentioned in the

Bible that establishes a link with his dreams and could influence how Joseph will respond to his brothers' visit. Of more significance is the fact that Joseph does not accuse the brothers of being spies in the Qur'an. We have seen that this is an aspect of the biblical story that raises a host of questions in the reader's mind regarding Joseph's reaction and the direction the narrative might take. Because he does not treat them harshly or level trumped-up charges against them in the Islamic version, the issue of Joseph's motives is less to the fore. The Qur'an account does not even mention the famine, thereby not fully explaining how it is that the brothers end up in Joseph's presence. It can be inferred from the text that the famine has spread to Canaan, but this is not explicitly stated as in Genesis.

A dramatic high point of this first meeting in the Bible comes when the brothers admit their guilt over the way they mistreated Joseph, unaware that the Egyptian official to whom they have been speaking through an interpreter can understand every word they say. When Joseph flees their presence and breaks down in tears there is a degree of ambiguity to his actions and the reader cannot help but wonder what he is feeling. The lack of such a scene in the Qur'an is a significant difference that does not allow the reader to focus as directly on the thoughts and feelings of Joseph and his brothers.

The Qur'an suggests that the brothers have provided Joseph with some of their family history, even though this is not mentioned in the text. His request that they bring their brother to him in v. 59 raises the question of how he knows about this other brother in the first place. The most logical conclusion is that there is a gap in the text that omits a prior conversation in which they tell him about Benjamin.

In the Qur'an, Joseph does not appear to be as determined to have a reunion with Benjamin as he is in the Bible. He warns the brothers that they will not be allowed back into his presence if they attempt to return without Benjamin, yet his actions and words do not betray a burning desire to see his younger brother. He does not keep one of the brothers imprisoned in Egypt in order to increase the likelihood that they will return. In Genesis this plan is devised after the brothers have been incarcerated for three days and Joseph has had a chance to consider his options and choose the strategy that will most likely allow him to see Benjamin. In the Qur'an, Joseph simply sends them all on their way, crossing his fingers that they will heed his order and return as soon as they can. His words in v. 62 make double use of an Arabic word (*la'alla*) that is translated "perhaps" and indicates he is not completely certain the brothers will follow his command and reunite him with Benjamin.

A comparative analysis of how the two texts describe this meeting between Joseph and his brothers shows that gaps can function in different ways depending on the nature and content of the information that *is* disclosed in a narrative. We can get at this by asking the question, "What is going on in Joseph's mind during this scene?" In Genesis this question is not explicitly answered, but Joseph's ambiguous behavior and statements suggest a number of possible answers to the reader. His harsh treatment of the brothers, his imprisonment of them, his decision to keep Simeon and send back the others to Canaan, and his tears all serve as clues in the text that invite the reader to try to solve the mystery of Joseph's thoughts.

The Qur'an's version, on the other hand, is a relatively sparse narrative that offers no such clues. The only thing the reader knows with certainty about Joseph's thoughts or feelings is that he recognized his brothers (v. 58), but the lack of ambiguity in his resulting actions or words complicates the attempt to interpret how that act of recognition is affecting Joseph. The reader is on his or her own and the text is of no help in filling in the gaps. Joseph's thoughts and motivation are even more mysterious in the Qur'an than they are in the Bible.

The next scene in the Qur'an describes the brothers' return to Jacob and his reaction to their request that Benjamin be allowed to go back to Egypt with them.

> [63]When they returned to their father they said, "Oh our father, another measure has been denied to us. Send our brother with us so we can obtain more grain. We are his guardians." [64]He replied, "Shall I trust you with him as I trusted you previously with his brother? Allah is the best guardian and the most merciful." [65]When they unpacked their provisions they found that their goods had been returned to them. They said, "Oh our father, what more can we ask? These are our goods that have been returned to us. We will bring provisions for our family and we will guard our brother. We will bring another camel-load of grain. That is an easy measure to get." [66]He said, "I will not send him with you until you make a promise by Allah that you will bring him back to me unless you are overtaken." When they gave their promise to him he said, "Allah is a witness to what we say." [67]He said, "Oh my sons, do not enter through one gate, but enter through different gates. I am of no use to you in anything from Allah. Truly, all authority is with Allah. I place all my trust in Him. Let all who trust put their trust in Him." [68]When they entered the way their father had commanded, nothing was of use to them in anything from Allah except a desire in Jacob's mind that He satisfied. Truly, he possessed knowledge that We taught him, but most people do not know.

The biblical parallel (Gen 42:26–43:15) presents this section of the story in a more detailed and drawn out manner. We have already noted that the discovery of the money in their sacks takes place in two steps in the

Bible: first one brother finds his at a resting place on the way home, and then the others discover theirs upon returning to Canaan. Similarly, it takes an extended period of time and several conversations before Jacob lets the brothers take Benjamin back to Egypt in Genesis. In the Qurʾan the description of these events is more streamlined, as both the narration time and narrated time are much shorter than in the Bible.

The difference in the way the brothers respond to the recovered money is interesting. In Genesis the discovery twice provides the reader with an opportunity to learn what is going on inside them. The first time they lose heart and turn to each other in fear (42:28), and the second time they and their father are dismayed at what they find (42:35). Their reaction in the Islamic text is nowhere near as emotional and revealing. "Oh our father, what more can we ask? These are our goods that have been returned to us." Without a hint of how the discovery affects them, they simply state the obvious. They understand the return of their goods to be some kind of sign to them, but there is a gap in the text regarding what the sign means and their reaction to it. Once again the Qurʾan is not very helpful in providing clues for the reader to fill in the gaps regarding the brothers' thoughts and responses.

The situation is different when we consider how Jacob is presented in the Qurʾan. He has been off the scene since v. 18, but his character exhibits the same traits he possessed earlier when the brothers returned home with the news of Joseph's "death." In particular, there is no doubt about the presence of Allah in his life and thoughts. He speaks four times in the course of the conversation with his sons, and each time he manages to refer to the deity at least once (vv. 64, 66 [2x], 67). His basic message is the same each time and is summed up well in his final comments when he says, "Truly, all authority is with Allah. I place all my trust in Him. Let all who trust put their trust in Him." He is a man of faith who is motivated by his beliefs and therefore remains confident despite the potential danger in sending his youngest son off with the others.

This is in sharp contrast to the brothers, whose motives and feelings are never fully articulated in the scene. It is also markedly different from the way his biblical counterpart is presented—a broken man who never mentions his faith and whose sole motive for sending Benjamin to Egypt is his desire to survive the famine that threatens his family's existence. This section of the Qurʾan ends in a way that shows Jacob is the focus of attention, and it resumes the theme of knowledge that has been a constant refrain throughout the Islamic text. "Truly he possessed knowledge that We taught him, but most people do not know." The implication is that Jacob's actions and words are informed by what he knows from Allah. The reason for the brothers' behavior is less clear.

The brothers immediately encounter problems when they return to Joseph in Egypt:

> [69]When they entered Joseph's presence he showed hospitality to his brother and said, "I am your brother so do not be troubled by what they have been doing." [70]When he had given them their supplies he put a goblet in his brother's saddlebag. Then a crier yelled out, "Oh people of the caravan, you are truly thieves!" [71]They turned to them and said, "What are you missing?" [72]They said, "We are missing the king's cup. Whoever brings it will receive a camel-load. I am responsible for it." [73]They said, "By Allah, you know that we did not come to cause trouble in the land. We are not thieves." [74]They said, "If you are lying, what shall be the punishment?" [75]They said, "He in whose saddlebag it is found shall himself be the punishment. That is how we punish wrongdoers." [76]He began by searching the other bags and then he took it out of his brother's bag. Thus did We plot for Joseph. According to the king's law, he could not have detained his brother unless Allah willed it. We raise the status of whomever We will. The one who knows is above every person who possesses knowledge. [77]They said, "If he has stolen, his brother before him did the same thing." But Joseph kept it to himself and did not tell them about it. He said, "You are in a worse condition because Allah is the most knowledgeable about what you describe." [78]They said, "Oh master, he has an elderly father so take one of us instead of him. We see you are a good person." [79]He answered, "Allah forbid that we should take anyone except the one with whom we found our property. Otherwise, we would truly be wrongdoers."

As in the previous scene, the Genesis account builds more slowly to its climax, but the Bible reader is given some indication along the way about what the characters, particularly the brothers, are feeling. They see the invitation to the meal as a cause for concern and they turn to Joseph's steward to plead their case (43:18-23). The narrator also informs the reader about the brothers' astonishment over the seating arrangements at the meal (43:33).

Joseph's emotions are revealed in Genesis when he sees Benjamin and is forced again to excuse himself so he may weep in private. The reader thinks Joseph is on the brink of disclosing his true identity, but he continues the charade. The Qur'an, on the other hand, presents a partial disclosure as Joseph immediately tells Benjamin who he is but withholds this information from the other brothers. In effect, one brother's gap in knowledge is removed while that of the others remains, setting up an "us versus them" situation with Joseph and Benjamin on one side and the remaining brothers on the other.

The Qur'an's description of Joseph's initial reaction to seeing Benjamin is typically terse and vague. Instead of being reduced to tears, the Islamic Joseph "shows hospitality" to his younger brother. What does this mean, and what light does it shed on his thoughts and feelings? Showing hospitality is a positive form of interaction, but it can be expressed in many different ways. The reader is not told precisely how Joseph treats his younger brother hospitably or what his state of mind is when he does so.

In addition to this, there is another obvious gap in the Qur'an version. What is Benjamin's reaction to the startling news that the stranger standing before him is none other than the brother who has been missing all these years? Like the Bible, the Qur'an gives no information to the reader about Benjamin's thoughts on this matter, but the latter text calls more attention to this lack of knowledge. As we will see, in Genesis Benjamin learns the truth at the same moment the other brothers do (45:1-3). Consequently, when they react as a group the reader assumes that Benjamin shares the feelings of the other ten. When he is singled out in the Qur'an and told before the others, the reader focuses on Benjamin and sees the events from his perspective, expecting to be informed about his response to the unexpected news. But this expectation is unfulfilled. The lack of any reaction on Benjamin's part leaves the reader hanging and highlights the presence of this narrative gap.

When the cup is discovered among Benjamin's belongings in Genesis, the brothers tear their clothing and circle the wagons in an outward show of fraternal solidarity. If one of them is guilty, they are all guilty and they prefer to stay in Egypt together rather than leave Benjamin behind (44:16). Their initial response in v. 77 of the Islamic text is quite different and takes the reader by surprise. "If he has stolen, his brother before him did the same thing." This is an interesting comment for several reasons. In the first place, it is highly ambiguous—which brother are they referring to? A logical choice is Joseph, although there is a problem with this reading since the Qur'an does not contain a parallel to Gen 42:13, where the brothers refer to Joseph as their brother "who is no more." How, then, would Joseph know about the other brother? If, on the other hand, the passage is taken as a reference to Joseph, it might be one of the few places where the Qur'an agrees with the biblical tradition that Jacob's sons did not all have the same mother. They might be claiming that Benjamin is guilty because of his biological association with Joseph the thief. By drawing a distinction between themselves and their dishonest brothers they exercise damage control and assert their innocence.

Another possibility is to interpret the brothers' comment about the "brother who did the same thing" as a veiled allusion to themselves. It may be a subtle way of admitting their guilt for the way they treated Joseph without being too explicit. If so, they are not separating themselves from Benjamin but including him among their ranks as one who shares their propensity to do wrong. This reading adds an element of drama and irony to the scene, since the brothers would be acknowledging their guilt to the very person they violated years ago. In fact, it would be the only place in the entire Islamic text up to this point where the brothers make any reference to what they did to Joseph. This is quite different from the biblical version, where they admit their culpability and even express remorse for what they did to him (42:21-22).

These are merely plausible scenarios that describe what might be going through the brothers' minds as they react to the discovery of the cup among Benjamin's possessions. Like the Genesis account, the Qurʾan does not divulge their thoughts or motivations, so the reader must try to infer from the information provided. The Qurʾan offers even less information than the Bible about what they are feeling, and this makes the interpretive process still more difficult.

The attempt to determine the brothers' motivation is further complicated by what they go on to say to Joseph in v. 78. One verse after explaining away Benjamin's theft as a byproduct of his family lineage, they attempt to protect him from the consequences. "Oh master, he has an elderly father so take one of us instead of him. We see you are a good person." The attentive reader will notice that the last sentence is a verbatim repetition of what his fellow prisoners said to Joseph in v. 36 when they asked him to interpret their dreams. In the earlier scene Joseph acceded to the request and explained to the prisoners what their dreams meant. But here he does not agree to release Benjamin, since that is not what a "good person" would do. "Allah forbid that we take anyone except the one with whom we found our property. Otherwise, we would truly be wrongdoers." Joseph has effectively turned the brothers' words against them. If he really is the good man they claim he is, he cannot do what they are asking him to do. But a question remains as to their shift from v. 77 to v. 78. Why do the brothers go from a flippant and cavalier attitude about the accusation against Benjamin to an impassioned plea for his rescue in the very next verse?

The answer to that question is found in what Joseph says in the second half of v. 77: "You are in a worse condition because Allah is the most knowledgeable about what you describe." Prior to these words the narrator says, "But Joseph kept it to himself and did not tell them about it." Joseph does not yet tell the brothers who he is, but he tells them he knows who they are, and this news gives them pause. In particular, his reference to Allah knowing about them catches them off guard. The reader imagines the brothers wondering, "What does Allah know about us?" and "How does this man know that Allah knows?" Changing plans, they propose a swap whereby one of them will stay in Egypt and Benjamin can return home to his elderly father.

But why do they make this proposal? Having one of them take the place of Benjamin undoes the penalty they themselves suggested in v. 75. "He in whose saddlebag it is found shall himself be the punishment. That is how we punish wrongdoers." Joseph's introduction of Allah into the conversation is the element that causes the brothers to rethink their strategy. They come to realize that this is no longer something between themselves and an Egyptian official. Allah is also involved in the matter, and the Egyptian apparently has the ability to know what Allah knows. It is their comment about the "brother who did the same thing" that led up to this, and the ambiguity inherent in that remark complicates the reader's attempt to discern what the brothers are feeling. If they were referring to Joseph, they realize that Allah has caught them in a lie since Joseph was not a thief. If they were speaking about what they did to Joseph, they now know that Allah knows of their guilt and, as Joseph says, they are in a "worse condition."

By proposing that one of them be exchanged for Benjamin the brothers may be going against the punishment they suggested, but they are also trying to fulfill the promise they made to their father in v. 66. "He said, 'I will not send him with you until you make a promise by Allah that you will bring him back to me unless you are overtaken.' When they gave their promise to him he said, 'Allah is a witness to what we say.'" It might be that when Joseph mentions Allah in v. 77 the brothers recall the promise they made to their father and they are now determined to do whatever it takes to keep the vow they made. In other words, they are operating out of a sense of both filial loyalty and fear of the deity. We will see that the next section of the Qur'an story supports this analysis.

Before we turn to that section, some further discussion about Allah's role in this part of the story is necessary. The frequent references to the deity have already been noted. The promise Jacob elicits from the brothers is made in the name of Allah, who is also a witness to the oath (v. 66). This adds a theological dimension to their entire trip: it is a journey that is made possible only with explicit acknowledgment of Allah's involvement and its success depends on the brothers remaining faithful to what they have sworn before the deity. In order to reinforce this point Jacob reminds them that Allah is in complete control when he advises the brothers on their itinerary in v. 67. "O my sons, do not enter through one gate but enter through different gates. I am of no use to you in anything from Allah. Truly, all authority is with Allah. I place all my trust in Him—let all who trust put their trust in Him." The truth of Jacob's words is established in the next verse when the narrator calls attention to Allah's supreme power. "When they entered the way their father had commanded, nothing was of use to them in anything from Allah except a desire in Jacob's mind that He satisfied. Truly, he possessed knowledge that We taught him, but most people do not know." We have seen that Joseph, too, theologizes the plot when he tells the brothers that Allah knows about what they have done (v. 77).

The most theologically significant portion of the narrative is found in v. 76 after the cup is found in Benjamin's bag. "Thus did We plot for Joseph. According to the king's law, he could not have detained his brother unless Allah had willed it. We raise the status of whomever We will. The one who knows is above every person who possesses knowledge." This section is noteworthy for two reasons. First of all, it makes reference to knowledge and plotting, two themes that have frequently recurred throughout the Qurʾan's Joseph story. The title "the one who knows" has previously been used in reference to Allah in vv. 7 and 34, and several times in the narrative the reader has been reminded of what the deity knows. It has also been stated that Allah bestows knowledge on Joseph (v. 22) and Jacob (v. 68). We have also noted the critical role that human knowledge, whether real or imagined, plays in shaping the plot of the Islamic Joseph story. This verse pulls together these different strands of the knowledge theme and presents the story's definitive statement on the topic: Allah, the one who knows, has knowledge that far exceeds that of any human being.

A similar point is made regarding the theme of plotting. Several times in the narrative Joseph is the victim of others who plot against him. His brothers (v. 5), his master's wife (v. 28), and the women of the city (vv. 33-34, 50) all function in this capacity, and the text uses the same Arabic verb *(kāda)* in each case. The final use of the verb is found here in v. 76, where Allah plots for Joseph. But this time there is a difference. Unlike those other instances of plotting, this plot is meant to have a positive effect on Joseph's life by reuniting him with his brother. It is also different because, unlike the others, Allah's plot will be successful. The presence of the two themes in close proximity to one another helps to make an important theological point, maybe the most important in the entire story: Only Allah's plots are ultimately successful because only Allah possesses true and complete knowledge.

The second reason why this section is noteworthy is that it is in the form of a comment from the divine narrator. This means that the reader alone, and not the characters, is made privy to the information that Allah plotted for Joseph and that without this divine intervention he would not have been successful. This elevates the reader's position and privileges him or her above the characters. The brothers, including Benjamin, have no idea why these things are happening to them, and the same might be said of Joseph since the text never states that he knows Allah has plotted for him. In effect the narrator's comment removes a gap in the reader's knowledge, a gap that continues to exist for the characters in the story. The reader has been provided with information that the characters will come to know only later in the narrative.

God in the Gaps (Qur'an 12:80-86)

Joseph's refusal to replace Benjamin with one of the other brothers means that they will have to return home and face their father with the dreadful news that he has lost another son. Before doing so, they take stock of themselves and acknowledge their own responsibility for the situation they are in.

> [80]When they had given up hope of (convincing) him they met in private. The eldest said, "Do you not know that your father has taken from you a promise in Allah's name and, before that, how you were remiss with respect to Joseph? I will not leave this land until my father gives me permission or Allah decides so for me. He is the best of judges. [81]Return to your father and say, 'Oh our father, your son has stolen. We can only testify regarding what we know and we cannot be guardians over what is hidden. [82]Ask people in the town we were in and the caravan we came with. We are speaking the truth.'" [83]He (the father) said, "No! Rather, your minds have led you to make up this story. Beautiful patience! Perhaps Allah will bring them all to me. He is the One who knows, the wise One." [84]He turned from them and said, "Alas for Joseph!" His eyes became white with grief and he was all choked up. [85]They said, "By Allah, you will not stop mentioning Joseph until you are completely worn out or among the dead." [86]He answered, "I complain of my sorrow and sadness to Allah. I know from Allah that which you do not know."

It was suggested earlier that Joseph's reference to Allah in v. 77 might have caused the brothers to recall the promise they made to their father and reminded them of the seriousness of that vow. This reading is confirmed in v. 80, where the oldest brother remembers the promise and reflects on its implications. He realizes they have violated the vow and he decides to stay in Egypt unless Jacob or a divine decree tells him otherwise.

The brothers, in the person of the eldest, undergo a significant shift in this passage as their self-perception changes considerably. For the first time in the story they express guilt and remorse over the way they treated

Joseph. They also have a more developed sense of faith in Allah than they have exhibited up to this point. The decision of the eldest to stay in Egypt unless Allah says he should leave and his reference to the deity as the "best of judges" reflect a level of belief that is missing prior to this.

Other than its presence in formulaic statements like "by Allah" (v. 73), this is the first time the brothers explicitly call on the deity and acknowledge Allah's authority. They are also less sure of themselves and their ability to pull the wool over their father's eyes. The directions the other brothers receive from the firstborn in vv. 81 and 82 about what to tell Jacob when they return are an admission of their limitations and an appeal to others to verify their claims. How different this is from the cocky know-it-alls they were earlier in the story when they thought they could manipulate their father as they pleased!

The reader is inclined to accept this as an accurate expression of the brothers' thoughts and feelings because the text states that they are speaking privately among themselves (v. 80). Their guard is down and they believe they are not being overheard. But this is only true in the world of the story. In fact, the reader hears every word that is spoken. This is a significant component of the text because it continues to fill the gap in the reader's knowledge regarding what is going on inside the brothers. The veil of secrecy has been lifted a bit and the reader now knows that two things are informing the brothers' assessment of their situation: a respect for Allah's authority and an awareness of their own limitations.

Here, too, a gap is removed for the reader while it remains for a character. Joseph is not aware of what his brothers say, and so he remains uninformed about their state of mind and their understanding of the situation. Ironically, it is his reference to Allah in v. 77 that initiates their process of reflection and soul-searching, but he is denied the opportunity to discover the effect it has on them.

In contrast, the Joseph in Genesis is made aware of his brothers' thoughts early in his encounter with them. After they have spent three days in prison Joseph eavesdrops on their conversation as they express regret for what they did to him and then interpret their present plight as a payback for the way they mistreated him (42:21-23). In other words, the biblical Joseph does not have the gap in knowledge that his Islamic counterpart labors under. In the next chapter we will see how this difference affects the way the reader views the two characters.

The narrative abruptly shifts location in v. 83, where we see a significant gap between narrated time and narration time. The description of the eldest brother's advice in Egypt on what to say to their father (v. 82) is immediately followed by Jacob's response in Canaan, with no reference to the brothers' journey between the two places. Jacob's initial response to them ("No! Rather, your minds have led you to make up this story. Beautiful patience!") is a verbatim repetition of what he said to them in v. 18 when they came to him with Joseph's bloody shirt. This use of repetition is an effective way of communicating the idea that Jacob is experiencing the same feelings that he had at the beginning of the story: faith in Allah and suspicion of his sons. The difference this time is that the brothers are, as they themselves say, speaking the truth, but their father has no way of knowing it. Once again the character's lack of knowledge about a matter known by the reader highlights the presence of a gap and adds to the complexity of the reading experience.

Jacob's words in this section are a theological tour-de-force in which he repeatedly stresses the supreme authority of Allah and, doing his part to highlight a central theme of the story, twice refers to the knowledge of Allah, a knowledge that has been bestowed upon him (vv. 83-86). The high concentration of theological language here and throughout this section of the Qur'an version underscores its relative absence in the Genesis account. All of the characters—Joseph, Jacob, and the brothers—refer explicitly to the deity, and each, in his own way, articulates faith in Allah. None of the characters in the biblical story expresses his faith in such an overt manner. In fact, in the 88 verses Genesis uses to tell this part of the story God is mentioned only six times (42:18, 28; 43:14, 23, 29; 44:16). In contrast, the deity is mentioned by name or title more than twenty times in the 28 verses of the Qur'an version, to say nothing of those places where Allah speaks in the first person.

These statistics suggest something about the different purposes of the episode in the two stories. The Qur'an account has a very clear theological agenda. The deity is mentioned frequently and the faith of the characters, especially the developing faith of the brothers, is to the fore. This is a story that is as much about Allah as it is about Joseph's family. The deity plays an active role in the events of the narrative and even speaks directly to the reader (v. 76). The biblical account does not have such a strong theological element. God is mentioned six times but is not an active character in the story and never says a word. Similarly, the faith lives of Joseph, his brothers, and Jacob are not a focal point of the Genesis text. The reader would be hard pressed to come up with a detailed description of their belief systems based on the information contained in the story.

Another way of speaking about this difference is to consider which relationships are primary in each version. In the Qur'an the divine-human interaction tends to dominate. By the end of the section each character's relationship with Allah is fairly well defined, and they tend to relate to each other through the deity. We see this most clearly in the case of Jacob. Before sending his sons back to Egypt he demands a promise from them with Allah as their witness, thereby placing their relationship with him in a theological context (v. 66). When they return to him with the news that Benjamin has been detained in Egypt he refuses to believe them and calls on Allah's help to reunite the entire family (v. 83). Even the sorrow and loss he experiences in his relationship with Joseph are understood in theological terms (vv. 84-86).

In Genesis it is the human-human relationships that are front and center. The key questions concern what is going to happen among the members of Joseph's family. There is no interest in the state of their spiritual lives and their relationship with the deity. The lack of any explicit reference to God's role in the narrative keeps the reader's attention squarely on what is happening on earth, not what is happening between heaven and earth.

This issue has a direct bearing on the gaps in the texts that are the focus of this chapter. The Bible and the Qur'an withhold a great deal of information regarding the feelings and motives of the characters. It is often impossible for the reader to know what is going on inside them, and their behavior is often ambiguous. But the Qur'an fills in a gap that remains in Genesis and complicates the process of interpretation for the Bible reader. The presence of the theological material adds to the reader's knowledge of the Islamic characters and gives a plausible explanation for why they speak and act as they do. As we can see in the case of the brothers, this does not happen all at once. In the beginning of this section of the Islamic story the brothers are mysterious and hard to read. The reader is unsure about what is going through their minds as they are told to return with their younger brother and they find that their goods have been returned to them (vv. 58-65). But as the story unfolds and the theological element becomes more apparent, some of the questions disappear and they are changed men as a result of their growing awareness of Allah's power and authority.

This is typical of the way narrative is presented in the Qur'an as a whole. The theological aspect of a text tends to dominate, and the plot is streamlined in a way that highlights that message. This is one reason why the Islamic version of these events is much shorter than the biblical one. The reader's attention is drawn to the religious meaning of this episode in the life of Joseph's family and all other details are secondary. In Genesis the theological dimension is secondary, and a comparison with how the Qur'an tells the tale makes this abundantly clear. Gaps remain in both texts, but the Bible reader has a theological gap that the reader of the Islamic text does not share.

One final gap worth mentioning concerns Joseph's character. When we compare the two Josephs we should not forget that the one in the Qur'an knows something his biblical counterpart does not. All the way back in v. 15, alone at the bottom of the well, he received a message from Allah: "You will surely tell them of this deed of theirs when they will not know." Because the Islamic Joseph expects to see his brothers at some point, he is not terribly surprised when they show up in Egypt unannounced. His reaction might be something along the lines of "at last the day has come!"

But the Joseph of Genesis has not seen the coming attractions. When the brothers arrive on his doorstep he may be in a situation he never thought he would experience. This adds an intriguing element of uncertainty and ambiguity to the unexpected reunion in the Bible. The gap in the character's knowledge leads to a gap for the reader. Since v. 15 of the Qurʾan text the readers (and Joseph) know that Joseph will not only encounter his brothers again but he will also tell them about what they did to him. This means that, in all probability, Joseph will have to reveal his true identity to them. When the brothers show up in Egypt, the readers expect this to be the outcome.

The Bible reader has no such expectation. The Joseph of Genesis has not been told he will ever see his brothers again, let alone remind them of the way they mistreated him. Consequently, the reader has no way of knowing what Joseph is going to do. Will he come clean and tell them who he is, or will he continue the masquerade? This gap makes the Bible story a much more suspenseful and unpredictable narrative. As the final act of the story begins, there is a sense of urgency in Genesis that is missing from the Qurʾan. What will Joseph do?

CHAPTER SIX

Endings: Joseph and His Family
(Genesis 44:18–50:21; Qurʾan 12:87-101)

Every story must come to an end. All narratives begin somewhere and finish somewhere, and we have seen that a great deal of artistic creativity is found in what takes place between the starting point and the end point. Earlier chapters have considered some of the ways authors go about the task of constructing a story. Characters are developed and events are described by the use of devices such as repetition, gaps, and the narrator's voice that build a world the reader can enter into and interact with. If the story is told well, the reader gets caught up and becomes personally involved. In other words, the world of the story becomes his or her own.

It has already been observed that an issue that often looms large in the mind of a reader is the narrative's conclusion. How will the story end? In the previous chapter we noted that the experience of reading a story is similar to that of being on a journey. The reader, like the traveler, is moving from point A to point B and is therefore heading somewhere. But there is an important difference: unlike most travelers, the reader is never completely sure of the destination. The reader is like a passenger on a train being driven by someone else, the author, who alone knows the final stop. Along the way the passenger picks up occasional clues about the direction they are traveling and what they might encounter down the road. But only when they pull into the final station on the line does the passenger know with certainty the end point toward which they have been moving.

That end point, the conclusion of the story, is usually where the plot's resolution is located. This is normally the way conclusions function in biblical stories: the central problem of the plot is typically resolved at the end of the narrative. The Joseph story is designed this way in both the Bible and the Qurʾan. The overarching questions that occupy the reader's attention throughout the story are whether or not Joseph will be reunited with his family and what will happen if such a reunion takes place. The reader of the Islamic text is given an important clue that helps address those questions: Allah's words to Joseph in the well suggest that he will in fact see his brothers again some day and that he will confront them about what they did to him. But the reader of Genesis is not as sure of the destination. As we have seen, even when the brothers arrive in Egypt the clues are ambiguous and it is not certain that Joseph will reveal his true identity to them. The Bible reader must wait until the very end of the narrative to learn what Joseph will do.

Because of the episodic nature of the Joseph story in both books, this is not the first time the reader has been confronted with such questions. The narrative comprises a series of shorter scenes with their own plots and resolutions, and each one grabs the reader's attention and draws him or her further into the story. Will Joseph have an affair with his master's wife? Will he remain in prison? How will Pharaoh respond to Joseph's interpretation of his dreams? Will Jacob let the brothers bring Benjamin to Egypt? Each of these questions, and others like them, attempts to resolve some problem in a portion of the Joseph story, but none of them continues throughout the entire narrative. Once Joseph overcomes the advances of Potiphar's wife, he (and the reader) leave her behind and move on to the next adventure. So, too, with each of the episodes.

Floating above all of these mini-plots and resolutions is the possibility of a future encounter between Joseph and his brothers. This is the issue that gives an overall structure to the narrative and is the main problem that must be resolved. From the moment Joseph's brothers sell him into Egypt the reader entertains the possibility that they will cross paths with him someday in the future. Each of the episodes along the way is another step in the march toward that rendezvous. Joseph's experiences with his master's wife, his fellow prisoners, and Pharaoh all set the stage for the main event that the reader has been anticipating since the beginning.

In this chapter we will consider how the two texts describe this culminating moment in the story. By now it should come as no surprise that the Bible and the Qur'an take divergent paths to reach that point. To further extend the train imagery, we might say that they make use of different sets of railroad tracks to arrive at the same destination. This was already apparent in the previous scene, where the Islamic Joseph divulges his real identity to Benjamin while his biblical counterpart does not do so. We will see that the two versions agree in a general way about how the story ends, but the conclusion the reader reaches about what the ending means is strikingly different for each.

One of the things the two texts have in common is the concentric structure of their plots. This is one of the most common ways of shaping a story. A concentric plot is one in which things end where they began. In other words, at the end of the story the reader's attention is directed back to the opening of the narrative. Sometimes this is a literal return to the place and setting of the beginning of the story. This is not the case with the Joseph story, since the narrative begins in Canaan and ends in Egypt. The return here is more contextual and thematic than it is geographic. In this final episode the entire family of Jacob is reunited for the first time since the opening scene. All of the characters are together again and the reader cannot help but think back to the start of the story before they were separated. In fact, we will see that the actions and words of the characters encourage the reader to make the connection between the beginning and end of the story. The same might be said about the thematic links between the opening and closing of the narrative. Several themes and issues emerge at the end that are meant to turn our gaze back to the first scene.

One of the main reasons authors adopt this kind of structure is that it encourages the reader to compare the two ends of a story in order to determine what has changed. Virtually all plots in the Bible hinge on a change of situation and/or knowledge, and a concentric arrangement facilitates the process of identifying and analyzing that change. Another way of saying this is that the characters are, in a sense, back where they started, but things aren't the same.

In this chapter we will be comparing texts in two ways. As we have throughout the book, we will continue to consider the biblical account in light of its Islamic counterpart. But we are also going to study the end of the story in light of its beginning as we pursue the issue of change in the narrative. In particular, we will attempt to analyze how the relationships among the different characters at the end of the story are different from what they were at the outset.

United They Stand? (Genesis 44:18–50:21)

After Joseph refuses the brothers' offer to become his slaves because of Benjamin's theft of the cup, Judah steps forward and makes one final appeal. His speech in Gen 44:18-34 is significant because it is the catalyst that brings about the plot's resolution. It is a lengthy speech, the longest in Genesis in fact, and its important role in the narrative merits its full inclusion here.

> [18]Then Judah stepped up to him and said, "O my lord, let your servant please speak a word in my lord's ears, and do not be angry with your

servant; for you are like Pharaoh himself. [19]My lord asked his servants, saying, 'Have you a father or a brother?' [20]And we said to my lord, 'We have a father, an old man, and a young brother, the child of his old age. His brother is dead; he alone is left of his mother's children, and his father loves him.' [21]Then you said to your servants, 'Bring him down to me, so that I may set my eyes on him.' [22]We said to my lord, 'The boy cannot leave his father, for if he should leave his father, his father would die.' [23]Then you said to your servants, 'Unless your youngest brother comes down with you, you shall see my face no more.' [24]When we went back to your servant my father we told him the words of my lord. [25]And when our father said, 'Go again, buy us a little food,' [26]we said, 'We cannot go down. Only if our youngest brother goes with us, will we go down; for we cannot see the man's face unless our youngest brother is with us.' [27]Then your servant my father said to us, 'You know that my wife bore me two sons; [28]one left me, and I said, Surely he has been torn to pieces; and I have never seen him since. [29]If you take this one also from me, and harm comes to him, you will bring down my gray hairs in sorrow to Sheol.' [30]Now therefore, when I come to your servant my father and the boy is not with us, then, as his life is bound up in the boy's life, [31]when he sees that the boy is not with us, he will die; and your servants will bring down the gray hairs of your servant our father with sorrow to Sheol. [32]For your servant became surety for the boy to my father, saying, 'If I do not bring him back to you, then I will bear the blame in the sight of my father all my life.' [33]Now therefore, please let your servant remain as a slave to my lord in place of the boy; and let the boy go back with his brothers. [34]For how can I go back to my father if the boy is not with me? I fear to see the suffering that would come upon my father."

One of the more interesting aspects of this speech is Judah's use of titles in order to define the relationships among the characters. Two titles are found repeatedly throughout. Seven different times Judah addresses Joseph as "my lord," a term of respect that is clearly meant to highlight Joseph's superior status. Further reinforcing this idea is Judah's use of the title "servant(s)" twelve times in reference to himself, Jacob, and the brothers. These twenty titles in the space of just seventeen verses are meant to underscore Joseph's authority and show him that Judah knows he and his family are powerless before him.

On the surface it appears that this speech is nothing but a rehearsal of information and events already familiar to the reader. Judah seems to be reminding Joseph about previous conversations they have had and filling in the blanks for him about what happened when the brothers returned to Canaan. But this impression is mistaken. A closer look reveals that the content of Judah's speech is not as familiar as it might at first appear. This is especially true of the dialogue he quotes. In fact, when we compare Judah's report of what the characters said with what they actually said earlier in the narrative there are very few points of agreement. The following list shows that throughout the speech Judah has taken liberties in his reporting.

- Judah has Joseph ask the brothers if they have a father or brother (v. 19), but Joseph never asks this question. Rather, the brothers freely volunteer the information as Joseph interrogates them (42:7-14).

- Judah has the brothers tell Joseph that Jacob loves Benjamin (v. 20), but they do not say this in 42:13. Similarly, their claim in v. 20 that the brothers have different mothers is not found in the earlier section.

- Judah has Joseph say he wants to set eyes on Benjamin (v. 21), but these words are never found on Joseph's lips.

- Judah has the brothers tell Joseph that Jacob will die if Benjamin is taken from him (v. 22), but they never make such a statement (42:18-25).

- Judah has Joseph warn the brothers that they will not see his face again if they fail to return with Benjamin (v. 23), but he says no such thing.

- Judah has Jacob balk at sending Benjamin with the brothers by speaking of the two sons of his wife, one of whom is no longer alive, and the horrible consequences he will suffer if they take away Benjamin (vv. 27-29). In fact, he does not respond this way in 43:11-15, where he appears to be resigned to the fact that Benjamin must go with them.

In each of these places Judah's report of what was said differs significantly from what was actually said, and in most cases he appears to invent entire lines of dialogue that are not found earlier in the narrative. But his memory is not completely faulty, since he accurately quotes dialogue in a couple of places. His description of the conversation between Jacob and the brothers (vv. 25-26) is a more or less exact account of what takes place in 43:1-5. He also accurately quotes himself in v. 32 when he tells Joseph how he will bear the blame before his father if Benjamin does not return (43:9). But beyond these two exceptions, the dialogue Judah recalls cannot be validated elsewhere in the text. He appears to be suffering from a case of selective memory.

In a situation like this the reader tends to view the character with suspicion. The biblical narrator is always completely trustworthy, and when a character says something that disagrees with what the narrator reported earlier the reader should side with the narrator's account as the more reliable of the two. It is conceivable that the disagreement is evidence of gaps in the text and that Judah is accurately reporting things that were, in fact, said, but were not included by the narrator. But the high concentration of such gaps in a relatively short passage, part of a text that does not elsewhere exhibit this feature to such a degree, suggests something else is going on here. The presence of dialogue that is accurately reported also argues against the presence of so many gaps and points in the direction of seeing the unsubstantiated material as fabricated.

Why would Judah distort the facts and invent a new version of what happened? An examination of the six portions of dialogue listed above suggests that Judah is embellishing things in order to persuade Joseph to substitute him for Benjamin, who can then return to Canaan. Furthermore, he is doing it in a most ingenious way: by subtly claiming that Joseph himself is the one responsible for the crisis now gripping the family.

In his re-creation of their first meeting Judah has Joseph insist that the brothers bring him Benjamin and then warn them of the consequences if they fail to comply. According to Judah, Joseph took the initiative by asking if they had a father or brother (v. 19), asked to see Benjamin in person (v. 21), and then told them they would not be allowed in his presence again unless they met his demand (v. 23). At the same time Judah reminds Joseph that the implications of his request were clearly spelled out to him. He has the brothers tell Joseph how much Jacob loves Benjamin (v. 20) and then inform him that Jacob will die if the boy is taken from him (v. 22). Judah also (mis)quotes Jacob himself about the pain he will suffer if Benjamin is not returned to him (vv. 27-29).

Judah is attempting to manipulate Joseph into letting Benjamin go free by presenting him with a revisionist account of their first meeting that places the blame squarely on Joseph's shoulders. According to Judah, Joseph forced the brothers to tell him about Benjamin and then demanded that they bring him to Egypt even though he was aware of the effect this would have on the boy's father. In fact, that is not how it happened at all. The brothers told Joseph about Benjamin of their own accord, and when he asked them to bring him to Egypt they did not utter a word about what Jacob's reaction would be. The narrator's description of their response to his demand in 42:20 is at odds with the way Judah remembers the moment: "And they agreed to do so."

This puts Judah's frequent use of the titles "lord" and "master" throughout the speech in a different light. Rather than being terms that reflect Judah's respect for Joseph's office and authority, they are better seen as being at the service of his real agenda. The titles are a way of ingratiating himself with the Egyptian and winning him over so that he can get what he wants. Judah is buttering up Joseph so that he will be allowed to take Benjamin's place and not have to bear the blame in the sight of his father all his life (v. 32). Judah hopes his speech will leave Joseph feeling partly responsible for the family's plight and therefore willing to release Benjamin. But his words have an entirely different effect.

Judah's speech is a turning point for Joseph's character because it contains information he is hearing for the first time. In particular, he learns some things about his father Jacob that he previously did not know. Judah tells him that Jacob has a special place in his heart for Benjamin, and his affection for his youngest son is so strong that he would no longer be able to go on living if Benjamin were taken from him. More importantly, Joseph learns for the first time about Jacob's reaction to his own "death" many years ago. Judah quotes the old man as saying, "You know that my wife bore me two sons; one left me, and I said, Surely he has been torn to pieces; and I have never seen him since. If you take this one also from me, and harm comes to him, you will bring down my gray hairs in sorrow to Sheol."

Although Jacob never utters these exact words, much of Judah's reported dialogue is echoed in what Jacob says elsewhere in the story. Upon seeing Joseph's bloody robe he reached the conclusion that Joseph had been torn to pieces (37:33). Similarly, when the brothers ask Jacob's permission to take Benjamin back to Egypt with them he refuses in 42:38 and says, "If harm should come to him on the journey that you are to make, you would bring down my gray hairs with sorrow to Sheol." Consequently, even though Judah has fabricated this dialogue it still has an air of verisimilitude because it matches closely what Jacob says earlier in the narrative and accurately reflects his state of mind as reported by the narrator.

Only now does Joseph learn of his father's reaction when the brothers returned home with the news that he had been killed. This had been a critical gap in Joseph's knowledge that prevented him from answering some very important questions. What did his father think happened to him? How did his father respond when the brothers returned home without him? Why did Jacob not try to find Joseph? Was his father aware of or, worse, an accomplice in the plot to get rid of him? The last question had to be a particularly troubling one. It was Jacob, after all, who sent Joseph to see his brothers while they pastured the flock at Shechem (37:12-14). Is it possible his father was setting him up? Such questions must have gnawed at him during the years he was in Egypt. They are now suddenly answered as Judah informs Joseph that his father has continued to mourn him until the present day. The information is more than Joseph can bear. Ironically, a speech that was intended to return Benjamin to Jacob now sets Joseph on that path.

> ¹Then Joseph could no longer control himself before all those who stood by him, and he cried out, "Send everyone away from me." So no one stayed with him when Joseph made himself known to his brothers. ²And he wept so loudly that the Egyptians heard it, and the household of Pharaoh heard it. ³Joseph said to his brothers, "I am Joseph. Is my father still alive?" But his brothers could not answer him, so dismayed were they at his presence. (45:1-3)

Judah's speech, especially what he says about Jacob, causes Joseph to come clean and reveal his true identity. The scene is such an effective one because of the different perspectives of the two characters. They each have a distinct point of view that colors and informs their reactions to the situation. In addition, Judah is mistaken about what he assumes Joseph's point of view to be. He believes he is standing before a prominent Egyptian official who is the second most powerful person in the land, and he cannot imagine why this busy bureaucrat would be interested in the lives of the members of an obscure Canaanite family like his own. He figures that by offering him a modified version of their first encounter and its effects at home he might be able to garner sympathy from the Egyptian and avoid the consequences he would suffer if he were to return to Canaan without Benjamin.

Judah is only partially correct in his assessment of the identity of the man to whom he is speaking. Joseph is indeed the second in command in Egypt, but this is not some obscure family for him. It is *his* family. The old man Judah describes as "your servant" is actually his father. Joseph hears the speech from a completely different point of view than Judah assumes, and the clash between their two perspectives is what makes the scene so effective and dramatic. From Judah's perspective the speech is meant to prevent future family problems, but from Joseph's perspective it begins to resolve the problems of the past. Hovering above both is the point of view of the reader, who is aware of each character's perspective and therefore enjoys an omniscience that neither Judah nor Joseph possesses.

The initial reaction of the brothers is one of stunned silence. "But his brothers could not answer him, so dismayed were they at his presence." This is in marked contrast to Joseph's tears and words, but the difference is perfectly understandable in light of their different perspectives. Joseph was aware of the possibility of a family reunion from the moment they first entered Egypt, but the brothers never saw it coming. At the same time, their silence is a sign of things to come—the text will not report any direct speech from the brothers to Joseph for the next six chapters. The one-sided nature of their communication continues in the next section, where Joseph does all the talking.

> [4]Then Joseph said to his brothers, "Come closer to me." And they came closer. He said, "I am your brother, Joseph, whom you sold into Egypt. [5]And now do not be distressed, or angry with yourselves, because you sold me here; for God sent me before you to preserve life. [6]For the famine has been in the land these two years; and there are five more years in which there will be neither plowing nor harvest. [7]God sent me before you to preserve for you a remnant on earth, and to keep alive for you many survivors. [8]So it was not you who sent me here, but God; he has made me a father to Pharaoh, and lord of all his house and ruler over all the land of Egypt. [9]Hurry and go up to my father and say to him, 'Thus says your son Joseph, God has made me lord of all Egypt; come down to me, do not delay. [10]You shall settle in the land of Goshen, and you shall be near me, you and your children and your children's children, as well as your flocks, your herds, and all that you have. [11]I will provide for you there—since there are five more years of famine to come—so that you and your household, and all that you have, will not come to poverty.' [12]And now your eyes and the eyes of my brother Benjamin see that it is my own mouth that speaks to you. [13]You must tell my father how greatly I am honored in Egypt, and all that you have seen. Hurry and bring my father down here." [14]Then he fell upon his brother Benjamin's neck and wept, while Benjamin wept upon his neck. [15]And he kissed all his brothers and wept upon them; and after that his brothers talked with him. (45:4-15)

In this lengthy speech, which is not much shorter than the one Judah has just delivered, Joseph offers his understanding of why he ended up in Egypt and the consequences it has for his family. The text ends with the statement that the brothers spoke with Joseph, but it does not record the content of their conversation. This is an interesting gap in the narrative that calls attention to the brothers' possible reaction to the discovery that this is Joseph. What is going through their minds as they process this incredible development? We can imagine that the only feeling that might be overriding their sense of shock is one of fear. Their thoughts must be racing as they evaluate their situation. "The brother we treated with contempt and scorn is now a man of incredible power and authority: what will he do to us? What have we said in his presence, unaware that he could understand our every word?" The reader wonders how the brothers can defend themselves, let alone wiggle out of this tight spot, but no answer is forthcoming.

All the text says is that the brothers spoke with him, with no indication of what was said.

Joseph's remarks suggest he is aware of the brothers' uncomfortable situation. After disclosing his identity he tells them not to be distressed or angry over what they did to him. This could be his way of assuring the brothers that any fears they might have about his desire for revenge are unfounded. But the primary motive behind his words to them appears to be to identify the one really responsible for his coming to Egypt. Four times in the speech he reiterates the point that God was behind it (vv. 5, 7, 8, 9), the first three times using the Hebrew verb "to send" *(šlḥ)* to convey the nature of the divine activity.

These are the most theologically oriented words from Joseph since he cited God's role four times in his interpretation of Pharaoh's dreams (41:14-36). Just as he understood the deity to be responsible for what was about to happen to Pharaoh and Egypt then, so now he sees God's role in the events of his own life. This is the first time in the narrative that Joseph has articulated such an idea, and it may be the direct result of what he has just learned from Judah. Until this moment he did not know if Jacob was involved in the plot to sell him into Egypt, but he now realizes this was not the case. As he reflects on what has happened to him in the intervening years, Joseph seeks some way of understanding all the good things he has accomplished despite the evil intentions of his brothers. He comes to the conclusion that there had to have been some other power controlling and guiding his life, and he reasons that only God can be responsible for the way things have turned out. The brothers thought they were ridding themselves of Joseph, but in fact God was saving him for the day he would "preserve their lives" (v. 5) and "keep them alive" (v. 7).

The flood of theological language in Joseph's remarks is matched by his torrent of tears as he cries on the necks of first Benjamin and then the rest of the brothers (45:14-15). A distinction between Benjamin and the others has already been noted in the narrative when he is given a portion five times greater than theirs during the meal with Joseph (43:34). Here Joseph privileges his full brother by embracing him first, before turning to the others. Benjamin responds in kind as the text says that he wept upon Joseph's neck, but it does not report that the brothers did the same. Instead of weeping, they "talked with him" in words that remain unreported.

The brothers' immediate reaction to this unexpected family reunion is to exercise a degree of caution as they try to gauge Joseph's motives and feelings about them. They remember the dinner party and Benjamin's extra portions, and now they see Joseph single him out again for special treatment. What is Joseph's agenda? Is he trying to lull them into a false sense of security only to exact his revenge when they least expect it? Their guard is up and they are not able to cry on his neck as he does on theirs. Their suspicions are heightened a few verses later when Joseph appears to play favorites again as he sets them on their way back to Canaan.

> [21]The sons of Israel did so. Joseph gave them wagons according to the instruction of Pharaoh, and he gave them provisions for the journey. [22]To each one of them he gave a set of garments; but to Benjamin he gave three hundred pieces of silver and five sets of garments. [23]To his father he sent the following: ten donkeys loaded with the good things of Egypt, and ten female donkeys loaded with grain, bread, and provision for his father on the journey. [24]Then he sent his brothers on their way, and as they were leaving he said to them, "Do not quarrel along the way." (45:21-24)

Once again Benjamin's portion is five times greater than that of the other brothers. The gap between them is further widened by Joseph's gift of three hundred pieces of silver to his younger brother. The twenty animal-loads of provisions that Joseph has them bring to Jacob further underscore his selective generosity, a generosity the brothers have experienced in only a very limited way with their total of ten sets of garments among them.

From their point of view there is cause for concern here as the brothers get mixed signals from Joseph. On the one hand his tears and theological interpretation of why he ended up in Egypt give them hope that he has buried the hatchet if it ever existed. At the same time the preferential treatment Joseph has shown toward Benjamin and their father with his concern and gifts makes them wonder whether he has ulterior motives. The reader, too, shares the brothers' uncertainty because the narrator gives no explicit information about what Joseph is thinking or feeling. The brothers are now physically reunited, but are they emotionally reunited with all the breaks healed? Hairline fractures may lurk just beneath the surface.

Joseph's final advice before sending them to Canaan ("Do not quarrel along the way") reflects an awareness that all is not yet well with the brothers. But here, too, the motivation for this admonition is unknown. Is Joseph genuinely concerned about them and giving them a last-minute pep talk before sending them home, or is something more sinister afoot? Perhaps he realizes their vulnerable position and the effect his privileging of Benjamin has had on them and he knows that if he tells them not to quarrel among themselves this is precisely what they will do. In other words, he may in fact be getting his subtle revenge by letting the brothers twist in the wind a while longer as they play the blame game and contemplate what might await them upon their return to Egypt.

The next four chapters center on the figure of Jacob and certain events that occur during the last seventeen years of his life. The material contained in this section includes the following.

- An account of Jacob's reaction to the news that Joseph is still alive (45:25-28).

- A list of the offspring who accompanied Jacob to Egypt (46:5-27).

- A description of the family getting settled in the land of Goshen (46:28–47:6).

- An account of a meeting between Pharaoh and Jacob (47:7-12).

- A deathbed scene in which Jacob blesses the sons of Joseph, Ephraim and Manasseh (48:1-22), and then his own twelve sons (49:1-33).

We will not devote much attention to this section of the story for two primary reasons. In the first place, significant portions of it, like the genealogical list of those who went to Egypt with Jacob and the description of him blessing his twelve sons, are not in narrative form. Consequently, they do not lend themselves to the type of analysis we have been employing.

Another reason why we will not discuss this section is more thematic. Once Jacob is reunited with Joseph many of the issues and concerns that had previously dominated the narrative are no longer treated. This can be seen in a shift in the focus of attention: the story becomes primarily Jacob's and less about Joseph. Jacob, also called Israel in places throughout the narrative, is the eponymous ancestor of the Israelite people, and certain parts of this section of the story describe what will happen to them in the future.

We see a good example of this in ch. 49, where Jacob/Israel blesses his twelve sons and tells each what awaits him. As their names suggest, each of the sons represents one of the twelve tribes of Israel and so this scene is meant to describe the future of each tribe. A similar concern can be noted in 46:1-4, where Jacob has an encounter with God before entering Egypt. The deity's message to the patriarch tells him about future events. "I am God, the God of your father; do not be afraid to go down to Egypt, for I will make you a great nation there. I myself will go down with you to Egypt, and I will also bring you up again; and Joseph's own hand shall close your eyes." The statement that God will bring the great nation up again out of Egypt is particularly important. It is a clear allusion to the Exodus, the watershed moment in the Hebrew Bible when the Israelite people escape Egypt and return to Canaan under the leadership of Moses. The

Jacob material at the end of the Joseph story is therefore more interested in what will happen in the future than in what has happened in the past.

But there is one final place where the narrative directs the reader back to the earlier part of the story in a way that suggests the brothers remain unsure of their standing in Joseph's eyes. It occurs after Jacob dies, when Joseph and his brothers return to Egypt after burying him in Canaan.

> [15]Realizing that their father was dead, Joseph's brothers said, "What if Joseph still bears a grudge against us and pays us back in full for all the wrong that we did to him?" [16]So they approached Joseph, saying, "Your father gave this instruction before he died, [17]'Say to Joseph: I beg you, forgive the crime of your brothers and the wrong they did in harming you.' Now therefore please forgive the crime of the servants of the God of your father." Joseph wept when they spoke to him. [18]Then the brothers also wept, fell down before him, and said, "We are here as your slaves." [19]But Joseph said to them, "Do not be afraid! Am I in the place of God? [20]Even though you intended to do harm to me, God intended it for good, in order to preserve a numerous people, as he is doing today. [21]So have no fear; I myself will provide for you and your little ones." In this way he reassured them, speaking kindly to them. (50:15-21)

Seventeen years after they settled in Egypt the brothers still harbor fears that Joseph will exact revenge against them. As long as Jacob was alive they assumed they were safe, but now that the old man has passed away they are concerned that Joseph will show his true colors and seek retribution. In a subtle use of repetition, the words "seventeen years" appear twice in the story, once at the very beginning when Joseph is described as being seventeen years old (37:2), and now at the end where it is stated that Jacob lived in Egypt for seventeen years (47:28). This *inclusio,* or envelope structure, causes the reader to reflect on the possible significance of the double use of this number. Perhaps it is meant to suggest a symmetry to Joseph's life with his father in which they enjoyed two blocks of seventeen years together that were separated by an extended period of absence and lack of contact.

Or maybe the number is meant to call attention to a connection between Joseph and his brothers. Early in the story they spent seventeen years together as siblings, only to be separated when the brothers took it upon themselves to "kill" Joseph and destroy the family unity. Now the tables are turned. Seventeen years after the family was reconstituted, the real death of a member signals another possible breakup. The difference this time is that it is Joseph who will disavow them and send them off to an uncertain future. What goes around, comes around. After spending seventeen years with him the brothers find themselves in the very same situation Joseph faced after spending seventeen years with them.

Right up to the very end, the brothers stay true to form. Their words, the last ones they utter in the story, are tinged with an ambiguity that causes the reader to question their truthfulness. When they return to Egypt after burying their father they tell Joseph about Jacob's request that he not harm the brothers for what they did to him. Several things about their report ring hollow and challenge its accuracy. Why would Jacob ask the brothers to relay his request to Joseph and not tell him directly? Why do the brothers wait until now, when Jacob is conveniently dead and cannot dispute their claim, to tell Joseph about it? Equally damning is the fact that the narrative does not describe Jacob ever speaking these words to the brothers.

It appears that the brothers are adopting a tried and true strategy in order to get themselves out of a potential jam. Seventeen years earlier, with their backs to the wall, they were able to manipulate Joseph by telling him something about Jacob that appealed to his love for his father. At that time their goal was to get Benjamin back to Canaan, but their words had the un-intended effect of causing Joseph to reveal his identity to them. When they now find themselves in a similar situation they resort to the same method and capitalize on Joseph's sense of filial duty by putting words in their dead father's mouth. As we will see, this raises some interesting questions about whether or not the brothers have changed in the course of the narrative.

Just as the first time, Joseph responds favorably to the brothers' at-tempt to manipulate him, but not in the way they expect. The reader is not told if Joseph believes their story about Jacob's request to do them no harm, but it is telling that he makes no mention of his father when he answers the brothers. Rather, he interprets the situation theologically and speaks only of God. "Do not be afraid! Am I in the place of God? Even though you in-tended to do harm to me, God intended it for good, in order to preserve a numerous people, as he is doing today. So have no fear; I myself will pro-vide for you and your little ones."

It is a brilliant response. He assures them that no harm will befall them or their families, but not because of what Jacob allegedly said. He will pro-tect them because of what God wants, not what his father desired. Without saying as much, Joseph tells them he is leery about their report about Jacob's request. It is a non-accusatory accusation. He will do what they want be-cause it is in line with his theological interpretation of the circumstances, not because they tricked him into doing it.

Once again a consideration of the points of view of the different char-acters sheds light on the reasons for their actions and words. The brothers still feel guilty about what they did to Joseph, and Jacob's death removes their only guarantee that Joseph will not act on any feelings of vengeance he might have. They cannot keep their father alive, but they can keep alive the protective role he played for them. So they concoct a story that is meant to keep Joseph at bay by exploiting the love and respect he has for his father. But Joseph's point of view is more complex than the brothers imagine it to be. While his feelings for his father are deep and intense, his primary motivation comes from his faith in God and his belief that the events of his life are part of a divine plan. Even though they get what they want, the brothers' attempt to manipulate him is ultimately unsuccessful because Joseph is looking at things from a completely different perspective.

Closing the Circle

The concentric structure of the Joseph story in Genesis is clear. The narrative finishes where it began, with Joseph and his family back together again as they were in ch. 37. The story concludes in a different location, but the characters and themes of the ending cause the reader to think back to the beginning when the family situation was similar. Similar, but not identical: As noted at the beginning of this chapter, one of the reasons authors make use of concentric plots is to encourage the reader to consider the end of a narrative in light of its beginning. In particular, the reader is asked to reflect on what has changed throughout the course of the story. We now turn to that task as we briefly consider each of the characters in the Genesis account.

Although he is a relatively flat character when compared to Joseph and the brothers, Jacob undergoes a change in both situation and knowledge. At the end of the narrative he has left his native land and relocated to Egypt. This change in situation is primarily due to a change in Jacob's knowledge. The discovery that Joseph is still alive and has invited him to move to Egypt with the entire family is what causes Jacob to make the physical change and leave Canaan.

Jacob is also the only main character in the story to experience a permanent change of situation by dying. Here, too, the circumstances of that change are markedly different because of Jacob's change of knowledge. As he says a number of times in the story, had he died without knowing Joseph was still alive he would have ended his life in a state of mourning and loss. But his death takes on an entirely different tone with his knowledge that Joseph is still alive. Rather then dying as a bitter and disillusioned old man, he passes away surrounded by all his sons, each of whom is individually blessed by the patriarch.

The brothers change considerably in situation and knowledge, but the effects of the change are hard to measure. They, like Jacob, are in a new location, but their primary change is seen in their relationship with Joseph. The young boy they were able to dominate and mistreat has grown into a man of considerable power whom they must fear and respect. Their concern at the end of the narrative that Joseph will seek revenge on them after the death of Jacob shows that they are aware the balance of power has shifted and Joseph now calls the shots.

This change of status is the result of their change of knowledge that Joseph is alive and has risen to a position of authority in Egypt. But what has this new knowledge taught them? Their very last words to Joseph suggest the brothers are still up to their old tricks as they resort to manipulation and deception to try and get their way. The false request from Jacob that they bring to Joseph is the functional equivalent of the bogus blood on Joseph's tunic that they brought to Jacob earlier in the story. The purpose of both is to extract themselves from a mess (the same mess, in fact) of their own doing by taking advantage of the feelings that Jacob and Joseph have for each other. Their method remains consistent to the end and the reader can only wonder if their change of knowledge has led to a change of heart.

Joseph undergoes more change than anyone in the story. In the overall scheme of things he is a more powerful figure at the end than he was in the beginning, but along the way he experiences a number of smaller changes that contribute to his finishing where he does. In each episode of the narrative he encounters other characters—his brothers, Potiphar, Potiphar's wife, the chief jailer, his fellow prisoners, Pharaoh, his brothers again—and each time he leaves the encounter a changed man. At the end he has gone full circle and Joseph is back to where he started, but he and everyone who has met him has been transformed in the process.

He also experiences a change of knowledge in several ways. Joseph learns that his father has been mourning him all the years he has been away, and this information removes doubts he had been harboring since he was thrown into the well. This information also serves as the catalyst that allows him to reveal his true identity to his brothers and resolve the main question of the plot. It is more difficult to determine if Joseph has learned anything new about his brothers and has experienced a change of knowledge on that level. The narrator does not reveal much about Joseph's thoughts and feelings regarding his brothers, so it is hard to gauge if and how his attitude toward them has changed. It was suggested above that he did not fall for the brothers' story about Jacob's request that he not harm them, and chose instead to absolve them for theological reasons. If so, this would indicate that Joseph gained new knowledge about his brothers' capacity and desire to manipulate others for their own gain.

The clearest change in Joseph's knowledge can be seen in his understanding of God's role in the events of his life. He becomes increasingly aware of the deity's presence throughout the course of the narrative. It would be more accurate to say that the reader perceives this to be a gradual process because the narrator presents only a selective account of Joseph's words and thoughts. In the early part of the Genesis story Joseph makes only passing references to God that do not speak of the deity's direct involvement in his own life. Examples of this are found in the scenes with Potiphar's wife (39:9), the prisoners (40:8), and Pharaoh (41:16, 25, 28, 32). Interestingly, the Egyptian ruler is the only character to articulate the view that God is with Joseph (41:38-39), but Joseph has no response to the statement. We have also noted that Potiphar sees that God is with Joseph (39:3), but the narrator does not say that Joseph knows that God is with him.

By the end of the story there is no doubt that Joseph views his life through a theological lens. The key scene is his self-disclosure triggered by Judah's speech in 44:18-34. It is a significant moment because Joseph not only tells his brothers who he is; he also tells them who God is. Joseph tells them that God is the one who protected him when they abandoned him, the one who, in an ironic twist, used the brother they tried to destroy as the means by which they would survive the famine. When he reintroduces himself to his brothers he simultaneously introduces them to a new way of thinking about their God. Such theologizing is not a part of his character earlier in the story, but it stays with him until the very end. Seventeen years after that encounter Joseph repeats the same message when the brothers return from their father's funeral fearful that Joseph will now retaliate. Instead, he reminds them that he has no intention of behaving toward them the way they once behaved toward him, and asks them, "Am I in the place of God?"

The book of Genesis concludes with a scene that describes Joseph's death and last words.

> ²⁴Then Joseph said to his brothers, "I am about to die; but God will surely come to you, and bring you up out of this land to the land that he swore to Abraham, to Isaac, and to Jacob." ²⁵So Joseph made the Israelites swear, saying, "When God comes to you, you shall carry up my bones from here." ²⁶And Joseph died, being one hundred ten years old; he was embalmed and placed in a coffin in Egypt. (50:24-26)

At the end of his life Joseph does the same thing his father Jacob did when he was on his own deathbed: He tells his surviving family members what will happen to them in the future. He informs his brothers, who represent the twelve tribes of Israel, that God will treat them exactly as God treated him. They will be brought from one land to another under the protection and guidance of the deity. His final request indicates that this will be an action that does not simply mirror what happened to Joseph; it will reverse it: the offspring of his brothers will bring him back to the land from which his brothers expelled him.

This brief coda highlights the concentric nature of the plot. The Joseph story ends looking ahead, anticipating a return to the place it began. That return will not be realized until centuries have passed and Moses fulfills his request (Exod 13:19), but with Joseph's final words the circle is almost closed. The coffin that contains his remains conjures up images of the young Joseph trapped in the well, fearful and unaware of the places he will go and the people he will meet. For now he remains in his tomb, waiting for God to act again and set him on the road home.

United, Not Just Reunited (Qur'an 12:87-101)

In the last chapter we interrupted Jacob's response in the Qur'an to the brothers' news that Benjamin had stolen the cup. We now pick up where we left off and consider how the Islamic text concludes the story.

> [87]"Oh my sons, go and inquire of Joseph and his brother, and do not despair of Allah's spirit. None despair of Allah's spirit except unbelievers." [88]When they came before him they said, "Oh master, poverty has afflicted us and our family so we have come bringing worthless goods. Please act charitably and grant to us a measure. Truly, Allah rewards those who are charitable." [89]He answered, "Do you know what you did to Joseph and his brother in your ignorance?" [90]They said, "Surely you are not Joseph?" He responded, "I am Joseph and this is my brother. Allah has bestowed favor upon us! Truly, whoever fears (Allah) and has patience—Allah does not waste the reward of the good." [91]They said, "By Allah, indeed Allah has chosen you over us and we have been sinners!" [92]He said, "No blame shall come upon you this day. May Allah forgive you—He is the most merciful of all. [93]Go with this shirt of mine and place it over my father's face so his sight can be restored. Then bring your entire family to me."

The Qur'an exhibits the same concentric structure as the biblical narrative by ending as it began with the entire family back together again in one place. But the way it reaches that point, as well as the overall impression it leaves with the reader, is distinctly different from the Genesis version. Perhaps the most notable difference can be seen in how the brothers come to know about Joseph's real identity. In the Bible the speech of Judah is the turning point that pushes Joseph over the edge and causes him to blurt out who he is.

There is no equivalent to that scene in the Qurʾan, where the revelation practically sneaks up on the reader. Actually, the word "revelation" does not accurately describe what takes place here. Rather than make a statement, Joseph asks a question. "Do you know what you did to Joseph and his brother in your ignorance?" The brothers respond with their own question ("Surely, you are not Joseph?"), articulated in a way that suggests they might be expecting an affirmative answer. Only then does Joseph acknowledge who he is.

Why does Joseph divulge his identity at this particular moment in the Qurʾan? He does not learn anything new from the brothers, nor is he overcome with emotion as he is in Genesis. His disclosure appears to come out of the blue and is not triggered by anything the brothers say to him. To understand the reason for the difference between the Bible and the Qurʾan on this point we need to return back to v. 15 in the Islamic text, where Allah tells Joseph, "You will surely tell them of this deed of theirs when they will not know." It has already been noted that this is an important verse for getting at the extent of Joseph's knowledge. Joseph knows that he will confront his brothers about what they did to him, and so he expects to see them again some day. It is easy to overlook the fact that Allah also tells Joseph (and the reader) when that confrontation will take place: "when they will not know."

This means that the timetable for when the brothers will learn the truth is not in Joseph's hands. Allah has determined when it will be, and the precise moment is at least partially dependent upon the brothers themselves. This is quite different from the way things unfold in the biblical account, where the timing is left up to Joseph. The immediate context of this section of the Qurʾan narrative indicates that this is indeed a time when the brothers "do not know." They say as much in v. 81 when the eldest instructs his brothers to return to Jacob and say, "O our father, your son has stolen. We can only testify regarding what we know and we cannot be guardians over what is hidden." This is an extraordinary admission coming from a group that up to this point has spoken and acted as know-it-alls. For the first time in the story the brothers acknowledge that they do not have all the answers.

Jacob also calls attention to the brothers' lack of knowledge in v. 86 when, after they mock him for continuing to grieve over Joseph, he replies, "I complain of my sorrow and sadness to Allah. I know from Allah that which you do not know." Indeed, ever since the brothers first set foot in

Egypt there is a great deal they have not known: that the Egyptian official is Joseph; that Joseph is the one who put their goods back in their packs; that Joseph reveals his identity to Benjamin; that Benjamin did not steal the goblet. In Allah's words, this is truly the time "when they will not know." It is therefore the time for Joseph to tell them who he is.

Before their return trip to Egypt, the last thing Jacob tells his sons is to "go and inquire of Joseph and his brother" (v. 87). They ignore their father's advice by speaking to Joseph only of the difficult straits the family is experiencing and begging him for grain instead of asking about their brothers (v. 88). Rather than respond to their request, Joseph resumes the subject Jacob broached with them by asking, "Do you know what you did to Joseph and his brother in your ignorance?" The nature of their offense against Benjamin remains unexpressed in the text, but Joseph's question keeps the focus on the main theme of the section by using two terms that highlight the theme of the brothers' knowledge. The light bulb suddenly turns on as they recall their father's charge to them and realize that there is only one way this man can know about what they did to Joseph.

Joseph informs the brothers about much more than just his own identity. His response is a veritable Who's Who of information about all the major figures in the narrative. "I am Joseph and this is my brother. Allah has bestowed favor upon us! Truly, whoever fears (Allah) and has patience— Allah does not waste the reward of the good." The brothers' ignorance is removed and they are finally know-it-alls in the best sense of the term. Joseph tells them about who he and Benjamin are in relation to each other, and he teaches them something about the nature of Allah. They also learn a subtle lesson about their father. When Joseph says the one who has patience will be rewarded, the brothers and the reader immediately think of Jacob. Twice in the story (vv. 18 and 83) Jacob utters the phrase "Beautiful patience!" followed by an expression of his faith in Allah. These are the only three times that words associated with the Arabic root that means "to be patient" are found in the Qur'an version. The brothers now know that their father is among those who will be rewarded by Allah.

It will take another few verses for the brothers to realize it, but Joseph has also told them something about themselves. When he says, "Allah has bestowed favor upon us" it is natural to assume he is referring only to Benjamin and himself, but this is not the case. Unlike in Genesis, the brothers' response to Joseph's self-disclosure is immediate and unambiguous as they point the finger back at themselves. "By Allah, indeed Allah has chosen you over us and we have been sinners!" But Joseph quickly assures them that there is still hope, thanks to Allah. "May Allah forgive you—He is the most merciful of all." The brothers now know that they, too, were included among the recipients of divine largesse when Joseph said, "Allah has bestowed favor upon us." In five short verses their knowledge expands in leaps and bounds and the brothers' veil of ignorance is lifted.

These brothers, unlike their biblical counterparts, openly admit their guilt to Joseph instead of trying to distance themselves from it. They do this because they share his theological perspective on their situation. In Genesis only Joseph sees God behind the events of his life; his brothers do not share that point of view. They fear that once Jacob is out of the picture Joseph will put aside the theological rhetoric and begin to speak the language of revenge. The brothers in the Islamic text are quicker learners. As soon as Joseph introduces Allah into the discussion they follow suit and interpret their offense against him in theological terms.

The theological focus continues to dominate as the Qur'an story reaches its conclusion.

> [94]When the caravan had left, their father said, "I smell the scent of Joseph even though you ridicule me." [95]They said, "By Allah, you are still caught in your old error!" [96]When the bearer of good news came he put it (the shirt) on his face and his eyesight returned. Then he said, "Did I not tell you that I know from Allah that which you do not know?" [97]They said, "Oh our father, ask forgiveness for our offenses. We have been sinners!" [98]He said, "I will ask forgiveness for you of my Lord. Truly, He is the forgiving one, the merciful one."
>
> [99]When they entered Joseph's presence he showed hospitality to his parents and said, "Enter Egypt in safety, if Allah wills." [100]He brought his parents up to the throne and they all prostrated themselves. He said, "Oh my father, this is the meaning of my earlier vision. My Lord has made it come true. He favored me when He removed me from prison, and He brought you out of the desert after Satan had sown discord between me and my brothers. Truly, He is kind to whomever He wishes, for He is the one who knows, the one who is wise. [101]Oh my Lord, You have given me authority and You have taught me how to interpret events. Creator of heaven and earth, You are my guardian in the world and in the hereafter. Let me die a submitter and join me to the righteous ones."

The first part of this last section of the Qur'an story describes a conversation between the brothers and Jacob that is a close parallel to the one they just had with Joseph. Both times the brothers utter the same phrase when they express their guilt, saying "we have been sinners" (vv. 91 and 97). In response, Joseph and Jacob use terms that come from the same Arabic roots to describe Allah as forgiving and merciful (vv. 92 and 98). Jacob's character has been remarkably consistent throughout the entire Qur'an story; he makes reference to Allah at every opportunity. Here that consistency is underscored when he repeats verbatim what he said in v. 86 about knowing something from Allah that the brothers do not know. By doing so he calls attention to both the brothers' relative ignorance and his own awareness of what the divine narrator has already told the reader in v. 68: "Truly he possessed knowledge that We taught him, but most people do not know."

It is important to note that in the Qur'an Jacob's character is not associated with themes like the return to the Promised Land and the future of the tribes of Israel as he is in Genesis. This is in keeping with the overall thrust of Islam's book, where there is no equivalent to the biblical notions of a unique covenant or a people specially chosen and set apart by God. The primary stress is on each individual's relationship with the deity, as seen in this passage where the brothers are concerned about being reconciled with Allah.

The final two verses comprise two brief utterances from Joseph, the first addressed to his father (v. 100) and the second to Allah (v. 101). His words to Jacob are a short theological treatise in which, like the Joseph of Genesis, he expresses his belief that the deity has been actively working behind the scenes in the events of his life. Joseph acknowledges that Allah has made his dream come true, released him from prison, and made possible his reunion with Jacob. He ends with a reference to Allah's knowledge, the central theme of the Qur'an story. Joseph's comment about his dream brings us back to the beginning of the story (vv. 4-5) and reinforces the concentric structure of the plot.

The story's concentric nature is also apparent when we realize that this is the first time Jacob and Joseph have spoken to each other since the opening verses of the narrative, and several things Joseph says here echo what was said in their first father-and-son talk. An example of this is the reference to Satan, a figure Jacob mentioned in v. 5 and who is also referred to in v. 42 of the Qur'an's version. The reference to Satan in the Islamic text is an interesting difference from the biblical account. In Genesis, Joseph states three times that God is the one who sent him to Egypt (45:5, 7, 8), so anything the brothers did to help achieve that result was in service to the divine will. But in the Qur'an Joseph acknowledges Satan's agency in creating animosity between himself and his brothers. This downplays Allah's role in permitting or being involved with the brothers' mistreatment of Joseph and places the burden of guilt on Satan. Such an understanding is in conformity with the Muslim belief commonly found in the Qur'an that Allah cannot be associated with evil in any way. This text expresses the theological position that human sin is the result of giving in to

Satan's temptation. It is a byproduct of human free will, not a part of the divine plan.

Joseph's description of Allah as "the one who knows, the one who is wise" also ties together the beginning and ending of the story because Jacob uses the identical titles when he speaks to Joseph in v. 6. The only other place they are found is in v. 83, when Jacob responds to the brothers' request to bring Benjamin to Egypt. In effect the use of the same terminology by first Jacob and then Joseph at the two ends of the story means that father and son are both speaking the same language and united in their shared vision of who Allah is and how Allah acts. This, combined with the brothers' newfound awareness of Allah's power and authority, means that there is a convergence of the theological perspectives of all the family members as the narrative winds down.

Joseph's brief prayer to Allah (v. 101), his last words in the story, also connects back to his conversation with Jacob in vv. 4-6. When he says that Allah has taught him how to interpret events he uses the very same phrase that Jacob did in v. 6 when he told Joseph about the many things the deity will do for him. This is simultaneously an affirmation of both Joseph's and Jacob's special relationship with Allah, the former because he has been given this special power and the latter because he knows how the deity will act.

Joseph's last request is an interesting one that merits some brief comment. When he asks that Allah allow him to die a "submitter," the Arabic term used is *muslim.* Several other biblical figures ask a similar thing in the Qur'an, but they are not expressing a desire to convert to Islam. The religion of Islam as we now know it did not emerge until the seventh century C.E., long after the biblical period. Rather, Joseph is asking Allah for assistance in living a life of submission (in Arabic, *islām*) to the one God so that he might be one of the righteous. According to the Muslim view, Islam was not a new religion but a return to the submission that was practiced by pious individuals like Joseph, Abraham, Moses, Mary, and Jesus throughout history.

At the end of the story the family is reunited in both the Bible and the Qur'an, but only the Islamic family is truly united. This is clearest when we consider the relationship between Joseph and his brothers. The biblical brothers have a lurking suspicion that Joseph prefers Benjamin to them and that he will eventually try to retaliate for what they did to him many years earlier. The first thing Joseph says to them after revealing his true identity is that they have nothing to worry about (45:5), but when Jacob dies seventeen years later they wonder if Joseph will now go back on his word. He does no such thing, and reminds them that what they intended for harm God intended for good (50:20). The text does not tell us what happens from that point on, but the more skeptical reader might well assume that the brothers never did get the message and spent the rest of their lives looking over their shoulders worrying about Joseph.

The brothers in Genesis never share Joseph's theological perspective on things. Where he sees God's hand at work, they can only see their own fingerprints on the crime scene. They never express mature faith nor do they ever acknowledge their guilt before God and ask for forgiveness. They simply do not see things in the same way Joseph does. They and Joseph are like two people who stare at a work of art and reach completely different conclusions about what it means.

The family in the Qurʾan agrees on what it means. By the end of the story they are all looking at things from the same perspective and operating out of the same mindset. It is a point of view that is shaped by their common faith and theological understanding. The text has repeatedly emphasized the theme of knowledge, both human and divine, and as it reaches its conclusion all the human characters share in their knowledge of the divine. Another way of saying this is that the characters in the Qurʾan are more interested in their relationships with Allah than in their relationships with one another, or we could say that they tend to view their relationships with each other through their relationships with Allah. The brothers label themselves sinners for what they have done, but both Joseph and Jacob reassure them that Allah can forgive their offense. The biblical brothers remain incapable of seeing their situation in these terms. They are afraid of what Joseph will do to them, not of what God will do to them. The brothers in the Islamic text undergo a profound change that they never experience in Genesis.

When we compare the final scenes we see that the description of Joseph's curtain call in the two texts also underscores this difference. In Genesis he asks a favor of his brothers and the other members of his family when, on his deathbed, he gets them to promise that they will transfer his bones to Canaan when God will allow them to return there. He is ultimately dependent upon others if he is to be buried where he wishes. That is not the case with the Islamic Joseph. His final words also take the form of a request, but he is not seeking human assistance. For this Joseph the important thing is not where he ends, but how he gets there. Accordingly, he turns to the deity, not his brothers. He wants to die a submitter and he knows that Allah, the one who knows, the one who is wise, is the only one who can help him do so.

AFTERWORD

We have responded to the Qurʾan's invitation to "inquire of Joseph," and the results have been interesting. The tools that narrative criticism and comparative analysis provide have made possible an interface between Joseph and Joseph that opens up new ways of reading and thinking about his story. The Bible and the Qurʾan share the same basic plot about the same set of characters, but the ways the two texts tell the story vary considerably. In other words, the two versions both converge and diverge.

We can best illustrate this phenomenon by imagining a situation in which Joseph would literally "interface" with himself. Suppose we were able to pluck Joseph out from the world of the Genesis story, sit him down next to his Islamic counterpart, and turn their chairs so they were facing each other. What would they see? As each one sizes up the other, theirs would not be the experience of looking into a mirror where one sees a perfect reflection of oneself. Joseph would not be gazing at a carbon copy or a clone. It would be more like the experience of twins who look at each other and see themselves as well as something else. Joseph would stare into Joseph's eyes and see the strong resemblance, but he would also notice the differences. This is not the same face that looks back at him from the mirror, and yet it *is* somehow his face.

The reason for the differences between those two faces is the difference between the worldviews of the communities that gave shape to the stories. The ideology of those who take the Qurʾan as a sacred text is distinct from that of those who view the Bible in that way. Each group has a unique understanding of the nature of God and how the human and divine interact. Each Joseph has been given features and qualities that reflect the worldview of his community.

Nonetheless, the family resemblance is there. It is there when the two Josephs interface, and it is there when the different communities that read his story come together. The people of the Bible and the people of the Qurʾan are, in a sense, just like Joseph and his brothers. Members of the same monotheistic family, they have often been kept apart by hatred, jealousy, violence, and misunderstanding. It is time for them to follow Joseph's lead and invite the estranged members of the family to the table so that the process of reconciliation can begin. Discovering how the two sides tell the family stories is a first step in that direction.

SUGGESTIONS
FOR FURTHER READING

Abdel-Haleem, M. A. "The Story of Joseph in the Qurʾan and the Old Testament," *Islam and Christian-Muslim Relations* 1 (1990) 171–91.

Ages, Arnold. "Why Didn't Joseph Call Home?" *Bible Review* 9 (August 1993) 42–46.

_____. "Dreamer, Schemer, Slave and Prince: Understanding Joseph's Dreams," *Bible Review* 14 (April 1998) 46–53.

Al-Qurʾan: A Contemporary Translation. Translated by Ahmed Ali. Princeton: Princeton University Press, 2001.

Alter, Robert. *The Art of Biblical Narrative.* New York: Basic Books, 1981.

Amit, Yairah. *Reading Biblical Narrative: Literary Criticism and the Hebrew Bible.* Minneapolis: Fortress, 2001.

Berlin, Adele. *Poetics and Interpretation of Biblical Narrative.* Sheffield: Almond Press, 1983.

Coats, George W. *From Canaan to Egypt: Structural and Theological Context for the Joseph Story.* Washington, D.C.: Catholic Biblical Association of America, 1976.

Cook, Michael. *The Koran: A Very Short Introduction.* New York: Oxford University Press, 2000.

Dawood, N. J. *The Koran.* New York: Penguin, 1990.

Fokkelman, Jan P. *Reading Biblical Narrative.* Louisville: Westminster John Knox, 1999.

Goldman, Shalom. *The Wiles of Women/the Wiles of Men: Joseph and Potifar's Wife in Ancient Near Eastern, Jewish, and Islamic Folklore.* Albany: SUNY Press, 1995.

Green, Barbara. *"What Profit for Us?" Remembering the Story of Joseph.* Lanham, Md.: University Press of America, 1996.

The Holy Qurʾan: Text, Translation, and Commentary. Translated by Yusef Ali. Tahrike Tarsile Qurʾan, 1990.

Humphreys, W. Lee. *Joseph and His Family: A Literary Study.* Columbia: University of South Carolina Press, 1988.

Kaltner, John. *Ishmael Instructs Isaac: An Introduction to the Qur'an for Bible Readers*. Collegeville: The Liturgical Press, 1999.

Kugel, James L. *In Potiphar's House: The Interpretive Life of Biblical Texts*. Cambridge, Mass.: Harvard University Press, 1994.

Matthews, Victor. "The Anthropology of Clothing in the Joseph Narrative," *Journal for the Study of the Old Testament* 65 (1995) 25–36.

Mir, Mustansir. "The Qur'anic Story of Joseph: Plot, Themes, and Characters," *Muslim World* 76 (1986) 1–15.

Neufeld, Ernest. "The Anatomy of the Joseph Cycle," *The Jewish Bible Quarterly* 22 (1994) 38–46.

O'Brien, Mark A. "The Contribution of Judah's Speech to the Characterization of Joseph," *Catholic Biblical Quarterly* 59 (1997) 429–47.

Powell, Mark Allan. *What Is Narrative Criticism?* Minneapolis: Fortress, 1990.

Redford, Donald B. *A Study of the Biblical Story of Joseph (Gen. 37–50)*. Leiden: Brill, 1970.

Robinson, Neal. *Discovering the Qur'an*. London: SCM, 1996.

Savage, M. "Literary Criticism and Biblical Studies: A Rhetorical Analysis of the Joseph Narrative," *Rhetorical Criticism* (1974) 79–100.

Stern, M. S. "Muhammad and Joseph: A Study of Koranic Narrative," *Journal of Near Eastern Studies* 44 (1985) 193–204.

Sternberg, Meir. *The Poetics of Biblical Narrative*. Bloomington: Indiana University Press, 1985.

Weinberger, Theodore. "And Joseph Slept with Potiphar's Wife: A Rereading," *Literature and Theology* 11 (1997) 145–51.

Westermann, Claus. *Genesis 37–50: A Commentary*. Minneapolis: Augsburg, 1986.

White, Hugh C. "The Joseph Story: A Narrative which 'Consumes' its Content," *Semeia* 31 (1985) 49–69.